What people are saying about this book:

"Get ready to start a wonderful assessment of your life. This book grabbed me right away, and made me excited to read the next story . . . and then the next! Congratulations Tim and Paul, the Seven Fs are an exceptional tool to create a roadmap to happiness and fulfillment."

—Joseph Otting,
President and CEO, OneWest Bank

"It's rare to discover a business book that focuses on the whole self. But it's impossible to succeed in business without holistic consideration of how you're doing as a person. I appreciate that this book doesn't just tell me what to do . . . show me what works for others and I'll decide what really works for me!"

—Beth LaBreche, CEO, LaBreche Murray Public Relations

"*What Really Works* is an agenda-changer! Paul Batz presented his message on blending the Seven Fs to the thirteen CEOs in my Vistage Group. All were so impressed we have changed the monthly meeting agenda for the first time in eleven years to allow time for each CEO to discuss what is really important in life: the Seven Fs . . . not just a P&L."

—James H. Anderl, Vistage Group 313 Chairman

"This project is starting a really cool movement. We all need help and encouragement to create the personal accountability to pursue the life we imagine. The Seven Fs really work!"

—Dan Mallin, Chief Operating Officer, Magnet 360

"I've been around long enough to know there's no roadmap for how to live your life to the fullest, but *What Really Works* comes close—a wonderful guidebook for destinations of the heart, soul, and an integrated life."

—Gary Johnson, President, MSP Communications

"Too many advice books are written by people who have had major crises caused by not living by their own advice. Paul and Tim live by the principles they have distilled in this book and are shining examples of how well those principles work when artfully applied to real lives."

—Stephen J. Haines, MD, Lyle A. French Chair, Professor and Head, Department of Neurosurgery, University of Minnesota

"There will be an eighth F after reading this book . . . 'Fantastic!' Thanks for reminding us not only what really works, but what is really important."

—Joe Schmit, KTSP TV Personality

"The Seven Fs give me hope and perspective about living a well-balanced life."

—Teresa Rasmussen, General Counsel, Thrivent Financial

"I've found the wisdom of the Seven Fs to be very inspiring. Since learning about this project, I've focused on my fitness and I've lost fifty pounds. I'm feeling great about my personal and professional life."

—John Driscoll, Executive Director, Hazelden

"I'm so excited to see this book come to life. Paul and Tim have pursued the Seven Fs passionately and intentionally. Wherever you are in your life, these stories will get you thinking and dreaming about the life you imagine and cause you to think about what's holding you back."

—Matt Norman, President, Dale Carnegie Training of the North Central US

"The Seven Fs are guideposts to help us achieve balance, as well as a sense of purpose. If you are open enough to consider some small, new, repetitive habits, you'll see a huge impact."

—Darin Lynch, Chief Liberation Officer, Irish Titan

"This book is great for those who have achieved much of what we thought was important and wonder, 'Why aren't I more fulfilled?'"

—Paul Dominski, EVP of Human Resources and Marketing, Park Nicollet Medical Center

"What makes this book a page-turner are the truly compelling personal insights of successful people. Their collective wisdom amazes, questions and inspires. Sometimes the roadblocks to your imagined life aren't obvious. Paul and Tim offer a simple but highly effective path to living one's BEST life."

—Sue Kilchenman, Owner/Vice President, BCT Minneapolis

"This is a great little book! It's a practical, easy-to-understand framework that ensures you are building your life on a balanced foundation. The Seven Fs help you set the goals needed to build a personal temple to last a lifetime."

—Mike Vinup, Vice-president, IML North America

"Paul and Tim are both powerful leaders who blend the Seven Fs in their own lives. Their stories are compelling . . . you're gonna love this book!"

—Jodi Harpstead, Chief Operating Officer,
Lutheran Social Service of Minnesota

What Really Works

Blending the Seven Fs

to Live with Less Stress, and Lead with Less Fear

Faith
Family
Finances
Fitness
Friends
Fun
Future

By **PAUL BATZ** and **TIM SCHMIDT**

Softcover ISBN 13: 978-1-59298-937-9

Library of Congress Catalog Number: 2010942067

Printed in the United States of America

Third Printing: May 2014

18 17 16 15 14   7 6 5 4 3

Cover and interior design by James Monroe Design, LLC.

Beaver's Pond Press, Inc.
7108 Ohms Lane
Edina, MN 55439–2129
(952) 829-8818
www.BeaversPondPress.com

BEAVER'S
POND
PRESS

To order, visit www.BeaversPondBooks.com
or call (800) 901-3480. Reseller discounts available.

Dedication

The most important lesson I learned as the Seven Fs moved through me was a comment from a friend who loosely quoted an Eastern saying: "Those who are building their dreams will never be angry or depressed."

The Western corollary could easily be, "If your dream doesn't work out, then get a new dream. Fast." I saw that phrase on a poster in a bookstore in Oxford, England.

We invest our lives in building relationships with people who cheer for us when we are racing, pick us up when we trip and fall, and be present in all of the joys and sorrows of a rich life. There are too many special people in my life to mention, except one: Thanks, Melinda. Thanks for living with an entrepreneurial author, speaker and executive coach. Who in their right mind would sign up for that? And thank you for asking me, "What are you thinking?" when we were in Ixtapa, Mexico. Through you, the Lord works in mysterious ways.

—*Paul Batz*

My grandfather from Chicago retired from full-time ministry at age eighty-seven. He was an amazing man—a pillar of wisdom, unwavering values, and gentleness. When life resembles a steep uphill battle, I often find myself asking the following question, "What would Grandpa do right now?"

"The best is yet to come" was his favorite axiom that's now been passed down to multiple generations in our family.

Today, hardly a month passes without some reference to Grandpa's ancient wisdom. For me, he is the deeply embedded anchor to which our family's faith, purpose and future are firmly connected. My parents, Walt and Lois Schmidt, embraced creativity and discipline as means of instilling these core building blocks for living.

This project has been grounded in my hope for two positive outcomes: (1) helping people envision a promising future for themselves and their world (2) unshackling people's inhibitions for better lives by providing a simple formula and real-world ideas for what really works.

My wife, Jeanette, is my ever-present stronghold. Every day she gives me hope for a promising future. Thank you for being by my side over the last twenty-five years and for the tireless support and unconditional love you've blessed me with. Truly, with you, the best is yet to come.

—Tim Schmidt

Contents

Acknowledgements

We gratefully acknowledge the insight and guidance of our Book Advisory Board:

Melinda Batz, Mark Bergman, John Busacker, Ted Contag, Ed Deutschlander, Kirk Gassen, John Geisler, John Goodrich, Jodi Harpstead, Dave Horsager, Sue Kilchenman, Christopher Kopka, Scott Lutz, Dan Mallin, Sean McDonnell, James Monroe, Tim Morin, Christopher Nelson, Kristi Olafson, Mark Peterson, Amy Quale, Teresa Rasmussen, Earl Rogers, Jeanette Schmidt, Randy Tofteland, Dan Wallace, and Magaly Wieczorek.

And our friends at MDA Leadership Consulting—where the Seven Fs concept was first articulated—who graciously encouraged this project.

We **don't believe** in the notion of **work/life balance.**

Introduction

We don't believe in the notion of work/life balance.
Mostly because the reference implies one is a sacrifice for
the other. Work is life. Life is work. Human beings were
made to enjoy working hard and building things.

But sometimes life is hard. We grow up being encouraged to follow our dreams and reach for the stars. We have
role models who have achieved *this much* by *that age*. It's
no wonder we set high expectations for ourselves and make
bold promises.

Yet at some point we struggle under the weight of our
obligations. For some, our mortgage(s), work deadlines, college loans and car payments delay magical vacations. For
others, our struggles are rapidly growing waistlines or
receding hairlines. Then there's the intricate scheduling
dance to help meet the needs of others—perhaps overachiev-
ing children or aging parents in declining health.

None of us are immune to struggling when important
parts of our lives get out of whack. We get overstretched. We
yearn for better paths.

A news headline in the summer of 2010 was startling:
"Survey: 40 percent of U.S. professionals want to quit." The
news was based on interviews with more than 15,000 business people in the United States. What were the professionals'
reasons for wanting to quit? Thirty-seven percent said their
jobs lacked advancement opportunities, 34 percent said they

were overworked and 31 percent said their companies had a "lack of vision."

Our lives are most satisfying when we blend together the most important elements of life. We call these the Seven Fs: Faith, Family, Finances, Fitness, Friends, Fun and Future. When these are properly blended we can live with fewer regrets and less fear. We can freely integrate the best and worst of our home and work lives.

Finding ways to blend the Seven Fs can be rewarding and encouraging. For instance, a female entrepreneur in her forties told us, "I've just now become comfortable in my own skin. I used to feel guilty that I was constantly thinking about my work. But then I realized, I'm constantly thinking about my kids and husband too! They've only known me as a woman business owner—that's who I am, and my family loves me as I am."

Another mom recalled a simple comment from her young daughter: "Mommy, keep up the great work!" Simple words of affirmation and encouragement help smooth the way to the life we imagine. Just as the Seven Fs have benefitted others, they can help you blend your world into a satisfying, sweet-life smoothie!

Our goal is to embolden people everywhere to set and live their lives based on the Seven Fs' blended life goals. We reached this conclusion on both micro and macro terms. People from every continent participated in the Seven Fs survey we created and used as the basis for much of the material in this book.

In the Seven Fs survey, more than one thousand adults volunteered their personal daily success habits about a particular F. One piece of encouragement about the power of the Seven Fs came from an adoringly devoted couple married for thirty-two years. After participating in a Seven Fs peer-group discussion, they turned off the TV, stayed up an extra hour that night and played Scrabble. Why? Because the life they imagined for themselves included more fun, but their idea of fun wasn't watching more TV. They pledged to play Scrabble every night they could.

Maybe Scrabble doesn't sound like fun to you, but that's not the point. The point is, too many people take life so seriously. Daniel Pink, author of the best-selling books *A Whole New Mind* and *Drive*, attempted to explain this phenomenon: "Self-help books used to exhort people, get them pumped up. Those days are over. There has been a turning of the page. People are looking for serious answers to help them navigate their lives." And that includes books like this one, which offers straightforward insights, tips and tools to help people live better right now. Why *not* Scrabble?

So, What Really Works?

How often is anything significant really accomplished alone? Even strongly independent people living alone build support systems to stay healthy and vital. The Seven Fs will help you articulate the life you imagine. Then you can surround yourself with people who share your vision and want to help you. That's what really works.

One of the simplest lessons we've learned from our efforts to share the Seven Fs insights of others is the positive power of mentorship. We've repeatedly heard from people who openly credit their success to what they've learned from mentors—and what they've learned by mentoring. One of life's greatest joys is finding ways for people to succeed together!

Over the past five years we have intentionally guided our lives based on the Seven Fs. We've challenged others to adopt the Seven Fs as their own personal and professional framework. The transformative power of the Seven Fs—for us and others—has been astonishing. Two anecdotes, one from each of us, illustrate what we mean.

Tim's Story: A Breakthrough at 30,000 Feet

"Where's home?" I asked a complete stranger sitting next to me in seat 20B on a West Coast flight.

"Seoul, South Korea," he muttered reluctantly in broken English.

After some prodding I learned "Jay" was attending three conferences. Jay, an internationally acclaimed retina surgeon with an MD in ophthalmology and a PhD in bio-medical engineering, was traveling to serve as the featured speaker at three prominent San Francisco-area university research centers to give lectures on his innovative work to other surgeons and researchers.

But Jay did not really wish to discuss health care or surgery. We connected when I shared I had lived eleven years of my childhood in Hong Kong.

He asked me, "What do you do?" I could have discussed my day job, but instead I said, "I'm starting to write a book about a blended and fulfilling life and how to create mentors who will help. May I ask you some personal questions?" He nodded and leaned in. My courage was rewarded.

INTRODUCTION

Jay opened up faster and far deeper than I had antici-
pated, and we shared a raw and emotional discussion. The
simplicity and universality of the Seven Fs helped two total
strangers connect as we discussed our lives. Seeking Jay's
highly educated perspective on my life, I shared with him
my life scores and goals based on the Seven Fs. As we discussed the cross-pollination of one F to another, he became
eager for the "now what?" part of our discussion.

As you might imagine from his professional credentials,
Jay scored very high in two of the Fs: Finances and Future.
In addition to his clinical practice and teaching, he was also
writing several college textbooks. Jay also scored high in
Faith. After overcoming severe diseases when he was young,
he felt the hand of God in his healing and decided he would
lead a faithful life by pursuing medicine as his career.

Sadly, Jay reported very low satisfaction with Family,
Friends, Fitness, and Fun. We discovered that his global
acclaim had also created a life distinctly out of balance.
Every day and most weekends, Jay works from a mind-
numbing 6 a.m. to 2 a.m.—with precious few breaks of
interruption. *Seriously . . . four hours of sleep?* I thought. I
looked Jay straight in the eye and implored: "Jay, something
has to change."

"I know, I know," he said. "But how?"

We worked together on Jay's plans for self-improve-
ment, based on the Seven Fs. Then in the real moment of
truth, I asked him to email me his improvement plan within
seven days—including who would serve as his mentor in
each area. Unexpectedly, he asked me to be his mentor! In
less than an hour of flight time, our relationship went from
complete strangers to mentor/mentee.

And more importantly, Jay's life started to change. He no longer envisioned his life through the single lens of his work. He had renewed vigor and optimism to embrace his life based on the Seven Fs. Read more of Jay's story in Chapter 2.

Paul's Story: What's On Your Personal Scorecard?

At 10:15 a.m. on a cold morning in January, I received a call at my office from one of my clients: "Paul, I need your help! I'm so glad I got through to you."

On the line was an executive coaching client, a sales executive in a *Fortune* 500 company that had just merged two businesses. Wall Street's hopes were artificially high for the newly merged firm. Together, we were trying to accelerate the integration of the two sales teams, but results were really suffering.

My client continued, "Our new president showed up at our sales leadership dinner last night unannounced. It was a nightmare. Instead of pumping us up, he hammered us. I've never experienced anything like it. He went around the table humiliating each of us one by one.

"So why did you call me?" I asked.

"I need you to come over and give our sales team one of your talks. Paul, I work with you as my coach because you keep me focused, optimistic and feeling good about myself. Can you be over here at 11 a.m. and do that for my team?"

I was dumfounded. In less than an hour, what could I possibly think of to say to this man's sales team? But over the course of a cold ten-block walk to the hotel where the

6

sales team was meeting, I wiggled into this approach: Do you ever ask yourself, "Am I falling behind or getting ahead?" And doesn't the best answer really depend more on your personal scorecard than on your professional scorecard?

Am I falling behind or getting ahead?

Upon arrival at the meeting, that's exactly the dialogue I shared. After some ear-splitting silence, the chatter broke through and I facilitated a conversation that lasted more than three hours. This group of Type A, alpha executives talked about their families, the condition of their minds and bodies, how much they meant to each other and the differences they were making in the lives of others.

Without specific prompting, what we captured from this dialogue turned out to be the Seven Fs. As our discussion evolved and we discussed each executive's personal hopes and priorities in the context of the Seven Fs the energy in the room brightened from gloom to gratitude.

The lesson of our dialogue was this: If we allow ourselves to narrow our feeling of success to our jobs, there will be days when we are living a fragile, falsely satisfying existence. By contrast, when we expand our thinking to include the dimensions of the Seven Fs and also take into account what really matters, our perspective becomes brighter. We become more emboldened to accomplish great things.

"What Can I Do to Help?"

The chapters in this book are shaped by real people, with real wisdom about the Seven Fs. We deliberately avoided quoting long-gone sages because when explaining to others the vision of this project, most people quickly asked us: "What can I do to help?" This led to a survey of participants and interviews with an eclectic collection of people.

So, here are the Seven Fs. When arranged alphabetically, they tell their own story.

Faith: Since the beginning of humankind, all cultures have included spirituality as one of the centerpieces of their society. Faith is quietly, deeply personal for some. For others, it's loud, strong and bold. For some others, it's self-defined. What role does faith play in your life?

Family: The traditional image of the nuclear family is being significantly challenged. Divorce, single parent homes and elders who are living past one hundred years of age are stretching family systems like never before. For most people, *home* is defined by having family around. What role does family play in your life?

Finances: Wherever you are, it takes money to live. For some, money is a goal. For others, money defines their purpose for work and a tool to fund their priorities. In many cultures, money can buy status—by both spending and giving it away. Eventually, we all deal with common financial questions: "Will I have enough?" and "How much is enough?" What role do finances play in your life?

Fitness: The positives of the mind-body connection have been made consistently since the beginning of recorded time. In the modern era of desk jobs, eat-on-the-go strategies and super-sized meals, we are wrestling with the cost of losing our collective fitness. What role does fitness play in your life?

Friends: The support we give and receive through friendships helps us live through life's surprises. Some people can collect and maintain a wide range of friendships even as personal and professional demands shrink their time. Others cannot. What role do friends play in your life?

Fun: In the Declaration of Independence, the pursuit of happiness (a synonym for fun) is listed as an "unalienable right." Indeed, when we are playful and joyous, our mood is contagious. We all benefit from spontaneous smiling, laughter and celebration. What role does fun play in your life?

Future: The sun always rises the next day. Progress and hope are the central concepts of future. We all have a need to improve our own condition and to believe we can improve the lives of others. Without the future, no one would care for today. What role does future play in your life?

Your Seven Fs Journey

The most meaningful moments of this project have been our conversations with real people. Through the Seven Fs, we get to know people at much deeper levels than we had ever imagined. And significantly, we help them pursue the lives they imagined.

Based on our efforts helping others apply the Seven Fs in their lives, we believe success with the Seven Fs requires the following:

1. Establishing a clear vision for yourself (defining your hopes or goals) based on how you perceive your life's journey.

2. Honestly self-assessing where you are today (using the Seven Fs worksheet noted on the following pages).

3. Wrestling with how and where you can effectively improve your Seven F score.

4. Finding the one key person (such as a spouse, friend or family member) who is able and willing to mentor you, help you be accountable for your development and share in your success!

This journey called life is so much more rewarding when we help each other. Young or old, near or far—we all need help dreaming without fear. We all need tough love. We all need open, honest, encouraging conversations about things that really matter. That's important for any relationship—at home, in the workplace, even at the grocery store. Thanks for letting us share the guidance of the Seven Fs with you.

Getting the Most from this Book

You are holding a collection of contemporary wisdom, gathered from people like you! This book helps you effectively reflect on where you are today and provides practical suggestions to help you grow.

1. Write notes in the margins. Literally. This book was printed on paper specifically chosen to easily accept your pencil thoughts.

2. Take the Seven Fs assessment today on the following pages. Then go to www.goodleadership.com to download the Seven Fs Wheel© and the Seven Fs Personal Leadership Benchmark tool—it's free. No registration is required.

3. Carpe Diem: Seize the day. Take action today to increase your positive momentum

www.goodleadership.com

Getting Started: The Seven Fs Assessment

To what extent are you leading the life you imagine?

Low				Medium					High
1	2	3	4	5	6	7	8	9	10

**Choose the number between 1 and 10
that honestly describes your own satisfaction
with each of the Seven Fs.**

	Low				Medium					High
Faith	My spiritual life									
	1	2	3	4	5	6	7	8	9	10
Family	My loved ones, who share a common sense of "home"									
	1	2	3	4	5	6	7	8	9	10
Finances	How money funds the priorities in my life									
	1	2	3	4	5	6	7	8	9	10
Fitness	The strength & health of my body									
	1	2	3	4	5	6	7	8	9	10
Friends	People who know me well & support my joys, disappointments & dreams									
	1	2	3	4	5	6	7	8	9	10
Fun	The part of my life that is playful and joyful									
	1	2	3	4	5	6	7	8	9	10
Future	The hope we have for ourselves & for others									
	1	2	3	4	5	6	7	8	9	10

Finding Your Momentum

Let's transfer your satisfaction scores from page 12 onto the Seven Fs Wheel.

A well-tuned Seven Fs wheel generates positive momentum in both our personal and professional lives.

Instructions:

Circle the number between 1 (low) and 10 (high) that indicates your current satisfaction on each of The Seven Fs on the wheel. Then, starting with the highest number, connect the dots.

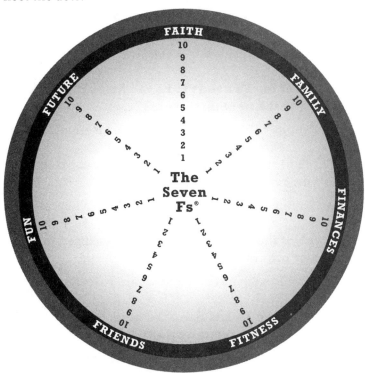

Will your wheel roll?

What shape did you create? Would you consider your Seven Fs Wheel well-rounded? How can learning to blend the Seven Fs together help you build stronger momentum? Answer the six questions below to build your strategy.

Download the Seven Fs wheel:
www.goodleadership.com

Creating Your Momentum

Circle the most appropriate answer to each of the following questions. The insights from your answers will help you increase momentum in your personal and professional life.

1. Which of the Fs needs to be the first priority for you over the next three years?

Faith • Family • Finances • Fitness • Friends • Fun • Future

2. Which of the Fs needs to be the second priority for you over the next three years?

Faith • Family • Finances • Fitness • Friends • Fun • Future

3. Which of the Fs do you feel most qualified to mentor others?

Faith • Family • Finances • Fitness • Friends • Fun • Future

4. Which of the Fs has been the most difficult for you to live up to your own expectations?

Faith • Family • Finances • Fitness • Friends • Fun • Future

5. Which of the Fs best describes how you think about your work?

Faith • Family • Finances • Fitness • Friends • Fun • Future

6. Do you feel more successful today, as a person, than you did one year ago?

Yes • No

About the Seven Fs Survey

More than 1,000 people participated in the Seven Fs survey. This page is a snapshot of what we learn.

The following chart articulates collective satisfaction, in rank order, among survey respondents. Satisfaction scores are based on a range of 1 (lowest) to 10 (highest). Most respondents were college-educated salaried employees or business-owners. Interestingly, scores were nearly identical between genders.

Fs, Ranked Highest to Lowest	Average Satisfaction Score
Family	8.06
Future	7.59
Friends	7.44
Faith	7.25
Fun	6.85
Finances	6.52
Fitness	6.06

Notice how fun and finances rank near the bottom for satisfaction—this is significant. Satisfaction with finances and fun correlated the most with overall life satisfaction. In other words, the survey respondents most satisfied with their fun and finances are most likely living the lives they imagine.

This book shares how individuals achieved success in specific Fs by making these Fs a priority. If your own satisfaction with fun, finances or any of the Seven Fs is lower than you'd like, we hope you'll be inspired by the input of others, willing to consider change and open to the idea you really can live the life you imagine.

At the very least, learning how to blend the Seven Fs into your personal and professional life will help you become more physically, spiritually and emotionally resilient—and that's only good!

Ready, set—grow! Let's get started now.

Seven Fs

Faith

Family

Finances

Fitness

Friends

Fun

Future

To say that faith is important in global and local societies is an understatement. The quest for a healthy mind, body, and spirit connection has been central to civilization since the beginning of recorded time.

One respondent to the Seven Fs survey joked that NFL football could be the eighth F. "It seems like more Americans worship football on Sundays," he quipped. That's cute, but actually, more people in the United States attend a worship service in one week than all of the people who attend football games for the whole year *combined*.

Faith is powerfully present in our lives. Out of more than 1,000 Seven Fs surveys, most people rated themselves at a 6, 7, or 8 for faith, on a scale of 1 to 10. Notably, three people contacted us personally to say they were turned off with faith as one of the Seven Fs because they considered themselves to be atheist or agnostic.

One took the time to call Paul to complain that he could see where our book was headed. "You and your buddy are going to rig your data to say that the only way you can lead the life you imagine is to believe faith is important," he said. Paul assured him the data would be reported as collected, with real stories about how faith is at work in people's lives. Then Paul asked, "What score did you give yourself on faith?" He replied, "I gave myself a 10 because I'm very satisfied in the fact that I don't believe in faith."

That story supports our conclusion that faith is intensely personal to people. And faith is powerful through contrasts: some people live a quiet, intensely private faith life. Others are into arm-raising, shouting, and singing celebrations of joy. Faith sparks violence in some neighborhoods and breeds hope and healing in others. Some search for nothingness, and others seek eternal glory.

Perhaps the most telling contrast to faith is how it can be an organized, public discipline for some and defiantly independent for others.

"I grew up in a very rigid religious tradition," a professional woman shared with us. "Breaking free from my parents' church expectations allowed me to embrace everything in my life to help me grow spiritually. I've grown so much by questioning the faith that the church drove into me as a child." She expressed her appreciation for the rituals and traditions she learned in her youth, but also explained her grown-up search to find faith on her own terms.

"Today, I feel more open, more fulfilled by asking my own questions about my faith and exploring the endless possibilities," she explained. "Following rules wasn't working for me. As I seek to raise a family, my husband and I are committed to building our faith together. We may decide we need the help of a church, and we may not."

Others find great strength and peace continuing the faith traditions instilled in them as youth. "My parents modeled an awe-inspiring faith-life example for me as a child," Tim shared. "It's a strong faith that has been bestowed on each generation of my family. I strive to live every facet of my life as an expression of gratitude because of God's gift of grace, love, forgiveness, and victory over death."

> *"My parents modeled an awe-inspiring faith-life example for me as a child."*

Tim grew up as one of three children of missionary parents and spent eleven years in Hong Kong. He was able to witness his parents' faith in action, through their work at the Hong Kong International School, and ultimately by helping Vietnamese refugees escaping to Hong Kong.

"Faith has always been my number one priority of the Seven Fs," Tim continued, "because it undergirds the other six. My faith is a spiritual compass providing biblical wisdom and direction for my life; guardrails to keep me from driving into the ditches of temptation; and a mirror for self-awareness, reflection, and humility.

"For me, this wisdom provides the art for living skillfully," Tim continued. "It's how we honor our parents, raise our kids, spend our money, go to work, serve and lead others, tackle emotions, and model peace. It provides a sense of grounding in a, at times, seemingly nonsensical world."

How Much Faith is Enough?

"I'm feeling terribly guilty right now," said a suddenly sheepish businessman. Why sheepish? Because the other men in the personal accountability group had just revealed their vulnerability. The date was October 2009—the height of the Great Recession. "Joe," by contrast, couldn't grasp our despair.

The coffee chatter was about how our businesses were sliding backward. We shared pains of strained personal and professional relationships caused by the pressure. Some in our group had eliminated entire departments of people; others gave pink slips to their personal friends. One man was walking away from his family business after selling it to the only bidder.

We groaned over telling our families that we were taking significant salary cuts—some with kids in college. Collectively, we were questioning our own value and wondering, "What's next?"

"Honestly, at age forty-nine, I have yet to experience anything like the nine of you have described," Joe said. "My career is going great. I just got a promotion. I'm feeling incredibly lucky, but I keep waiting for something really bad to happen to me . . . not because I want it, but I want to know if I have enough faith to handle something really difficult."

What did Joe mean by "enough faith"? For that matter, what is faith?

Intense Beliefs

"Most faith disciplines recognize that humans are inherently spiritual beings, who are inclined to believe things deeply. I believe that faith is an intense heart commitment to something or someone bigger than myself," explained Bruce Pinke, a scholar who writes, teaches, and lectures on the connection between Christianity and the other major faith disciplines.

Throughout thirty years of working with multifaith leaders around the globe, Pinke has grown to see that the dominant faiths have much in common:

- Their search for meaning and significance within their world

- Their hope/trust in the inherent potential of human goodness

- An attitude of gratitude and thankfulness for life

According to Pinke, there are basic questions we all seem to share, regardless of our faith structure:

- Where did I come from?

- Why am I here right now?

- What happens after death?

"Through my experiences, I have seen that wrestling with these questions helps people to live more purposefully and with courage in the face of life's inevitable hardships," Pinke said. He also noted that people of strong faith invest themselves in the lives and causes of others, and thus discover their own place in the universal community.

Faith Forged by Fire

With some people, faith has been forged through their personal experiences. "I'm not at all worried about tomorrow," said Chady AlAhmar, a strategist for a *Fortune* 500 financial firm. "I grew up in Lebanon, where my family was literally caught in the cross-fire of a senseless street war."

Of the many atrocities he experienced as a child, AlAhmar shared that when he was fourteen years old, his family hid from the violence by living underground in a home's cellar. His father snuck out once a day, successfully evading bombs and snipers to retrieve food, water, and fresh information.

After three months of living in the cellar, AlAhmar's family decided to emerge into the daylight and flee the conflict area—after learning enough about the pattern of the snipers.

They literally prayed the snipers would give them a pass.

"My dad said it was too risky for us to flee in one car. Even though I had never driven before, I looked my dad in the eye and said, 'I can drive,'" AlAhmar said. The family escaped by racing through the streets with white flags flapping from the car's windows. They literally prayed the snipers would give them a pass.

Once they arrived on safer ground, AlAhmar's parents sent him to France for a Western education. He then came to America with nothing but his academic diplomas. "Although still emotionally scarred, I honestly believe our faith is what guided us out of danger in Lebanon and helped me seek a better life," he said.

"Today, I know my place on earth is to raise a healthy, confident family who will make a difference in this world," AlAhmar continued. "I want my wife and kids to truly understand how fortunate we are to live in peace and to have such wonderful opportunities. From my childhood experiences, I look at my life through a strong faith lens: with what I lived through, how can anything else be that bad?"

Believing in People

A religious scholar who taught the fundamentals of faith integration challenged his students with this philosophical dilemma:

> Let's suppose that a hurricane with high winds and flooding destroyed a mosque in your community. Would you give your time, money, and prayers to help rebuild it, even if you were not Muslim? Why or why not? What does your faith call you to do?

The point of the exercise is to tap the inherent sense of goodness in our faith perspectives—to bring to the surface the potential goodness of our fellow humans. Most students wrestle with the dilemma and decide that basic human dignity and respect win out over their sense of what's right or wrong based on their own faith doctrines.

That type of faith wrestling is playing out daily in a variety of neighborhoods and communities, based on the input of the many people we interviewed. The melting pot of international cultures is getting thicker as people of differing faiths learn to appreciate one another.

For example, Ertugrul Tuzcu was raised in a Muslim household in Turkey. With his family's encouragement, he came to the United States for an engineering education at a major university. He built a prosperous career in retailing and raised a beautiful family with an American-born wife who is Christian. Given the disparity of their native faiths, Tuzcu explained a moment of clarity and joy when he and his spouse felt united in their beliefs.

"Recently, my wife and I worshipped in a church community that made us both feel welcome," Tuzcu explained. "The sanctuary had no cross. Their message was that the holy spirit was within the people in the pew, not hanging on the wall. We found ourselves coming together in our faiths, feeling welcomed and motivated."

For Christian Isquierdo and his wife, Heather, their faith journey had perhaps been predestined for years.

The Isquierdos met as graduate students at Naropa University in Boulder, Colorado. Naropa was the United States' first accredited Buddhist university, and Heather and Christian were both drawn to the same Eastern Buddhist teachings.

"I was raised by wonderful parents who believed it was up to me to find my own spiritual path," Heather explained. Christian, on the other hand, attended a Catholic school as a child, but did not ascribe to all of its practices and rituals. He peacefully declined the school's confirmation ceremonies. "My school administrators and friends weren't too happy with me," he laughed.

As the Isquierdos prepared to send their oldest child to school, they selected a private Catholic school in their neighborhood. "We feel our blended beliefs can coexist. We like the structured learning of the Catholic school, and we think it's good for our family to be a part of a faith community," Christian said.

For businessman Dan Lieberman, his Jewish faith is a centerpiece of his life and work in building a strong community. He explained, "We have a fourth-generation private business that's been serving customers and caring for employees for more than one hundred years in the same community. My family's Jewish faith traditions are the foundation for our core company values."

"You can't be a jerk at the office and ask for forgiveness at the synagogue."

Professionally and personally, Lieberman is a firm believer in the Golden Rule—treat other people the way you want to be treated. "To thrive over such a long period of time, we have to live and work with transparency," he said. "You can't be a jerk at the office and ask for forgiveness at the synagogue. It's just doesn't work that way."

Specifically, there are two uniquely Jewish influences that undergird Lieberman's success. First is the concept of *Tzedakah*. "Giving to charity is a part of Tzedakah, but it's deeper than that," Lieberman said. "We believe we have an obligation to build a strong community by taking care of the poor."

That value comes alive in an award-winning United Way fundraising campaign organized by Lieberman's company that directly involves employees and customers. "We get our employees involved in planning a really big United Way week every year with raffles, a silent auction, and contests on video games," he explained. "It's a great way for our employees to see one of our core values in action, and for such a good cause."

Lieberman also noted the importance of honoring the Sabbath as a vital strategy for him to stay centered around his faith and family. "The Jewish Sabbath is from Friday at sundown through Saturday at sundown," he explained. "In the strictest interpretations, Jews do not drive, cook, or even light a match. In our family, we try as hard as we can to have a family meal on Friday night, so we can stay connected. And I try to stay away from email and voicemail from Friday after work until sometime on Sunday. It helps me stay fresh and motivated about my work when I unplug from the office during the Sabbath every week."

Ram Ramakrishnan and his wife, Shanti, are living their Hindu faith in the context of many life transitions and challenges. They came from India, which is about 80 percent Hindu, to the United States, where less than 1 percent of the population is Hindu. The family's geographic change has also meant cultural changes. Ramakrishnan explained one contrast: "Friday is the holy day in our faith tradition, but in our American lives, we have to work on Fridays."

Still, the Ramakrishnans are satisfied with the changes they have made and seek to give back within the community where they reside. "Goodness is a deeply held value for my family," Ram explained. "We follow the thought that we are obligated to a life of doing good things. We do not expect that all good things will bear results in our lives now, but it will come back in many ways."

God at Work

In 2002, Lawrence Research, a firm based in Santa Ana, California, was commissioned to execute a survey called "The State of Faith." The firm interviewed a multi-faith random sample of five hundred business executives in the United States on the subject of faith.

The study found that faith played a strong role in helping most executives handle the difficulty of their roles as leaders:

1. Seventy-four percent said they would "pray for help or inspiration" when facing a difficult decision.

2. Seventy-two percent claimed to have prayed at work by themselves.

3. Thirty percent prayed at work with others.

What are these executives typically praying for? The survey didn't ask, but Richard Davis, CEO of US Bank, shared his personal insight on the subject. Davis, head of one of the nation's largest banks, was among the banking executives President Obama called to the White House in the midst of the Banking Crisis in 2009.

He and a select list of other top bank executives gathered outside the Oval Office for their meeting with the leader of the United States. Tensions in the banking community were high. The White House seemed intent on portraying the banks as wrongdoers, and the air was ripe for high-level finger pointing. Davis remembers at that moment choosing to pray for strength and collaboration.

"My faith provides a foundation for me to not have to win all the time," he explained. "For me, I've learned it's always best to listen for ways everyone can succeed. That day outside the Oval Office, I prayed for the collective self-control of the group to recognize that we were all good people and well-intentioned leaders. I asked our God to help us listen and negotiate with respect."

The bankers' meeting with the president and his top aides was a turning point in establishing a new tone that led to progress in restoring trust in the American banking system.

Giving Thanks

Sometimes, as we all know, life is hard. The frailties of our lives include any number of heartaches, disappointments, betrayals, and hard lessons. Many of our interviews revealed that simple, quiet introspection is a profound source of healing, renewal, and growth.

"Simply the awareness of being in the presence of God can help you be grateful for wherever you happen to be right at that moment," explained Tim Morin, a marketing vice president by day and an insightful, inspirational author and blogger in his free time.

One year, Morin gave up consuming media—no news or noise—for the forty days of Lent before Easter. He found that consistently listening to his soul without hearing the negative dialogue of the media was liberating.

To those who similarly seek such quietude, he offered this advice: "In the quiet of your own soul, honestly, courageously, and humbly reflect on areas of your day where you have noticed, felt, and sensed life-giving energy, or perhaps moments of consolation or peacefulness. Also, reflect on those areas or moments where you have felt dry, agitated, fearful, or otherwise out of sorts."

"And that's it," Morin said. "Simply take from this exercise honest acknowledgement of the movements working within you. No need for immediate judgment or harsh self-criticism or hasty decisions to act, unless you decide it is time to do so."

Humility fueled by strong faith can help us avoid becoming negative during the inevitable stresses of our lives. Paul recalls witnessing a pointed moment of gratitude when watching videos of people who endured a one-hundred-year flood in the Red River Valley of North Dakota. More than half of the homes in the Grand Forks community were consumed by muddy floodwaters.

"I can see the face of God in the men who are shoveling mud out of my basement."

"I was struck by the faithful response from an elderly woman in a shelter. She could have been so angry and bitter," Paul explained. "Instead, when asked, 'What sense can you make of all this?' she replied, 'I can see the face of God in the men who are shoveling mud out of my basement. Where would I be without them? I am so grateful for the loving care and attention we receive.'"

Achieve or Receive?

At our core, no matter our faith structure, we don't think any of us achieve anything significant in our lives on our own accord. If we live with faith-instilled gratitude, we can see that we actually receive the benefits that others create for us.

Ask yourself, "What do I have in my life that I have not received—directly or indirectly—from others?" Trust, love, respect, money, responsibility, challenges—strong faith helps us to see everything in life as a gift. In short, gratitude helps us to lead our lives with a healthier attitude.

With so many hard-working people seeking a stronger faith life, leaders have the opportunity to include faith more often in the business dialogue. Leaders very publicly bring faith to their followers in times of personal or professional crises, when comforting a colleague in distress, or when explaining a natural disaster. Leaders can also demonstrate faith more consistently by talking frequently about their core values and how their faith guides their decisions.

How can stronger faith improve your satisfaction and propel you toward the life you imagine?

SUCCESS HABIT: Faith

I have learned to crave my private time when I swim for exercise. I swim at least fifty-two lengths of the pool, praying the alphabet along the way. My first length, I pray for something that begins with the letter A, then B, and so on. Fifty-two laps is twice around the alphabet. It's a great workout for my body and soul.

SUCCESS HABIT: Faith

We have found that volunteering as a family always deepens our faith. We have the attitude that we would rather see a sermon than hear one any day. Our faith calls us to good works. When we help others, we feel so much better about ourselves and stronger in our faith. The eye is a better pupil and more willing than the ear.

SUCCESS HABIT: Faith

At Thanksgiving every year, we host a group of family and friends. After dinner, we go around the table and make a list of the people in our lives who are blessings. Some years, we spend more than an hour making the list. Then, when we're done, we all agree to write a note to one of the people on our list and send a small donation to our church in their name. Now, our children are starting to do this with their own children . . . we are so grateful.

Seven Fs

Faith
Family
Finances
Fitness
Friends
Fun
Future

Tim learned a lot about the importance of his family one night in Hong Kong. "A police officer escorted a friend and me off the #6 double-decker bus into his squad car to be booked into the local Hong Kong jail," he recalled. "It was terrifying."

Tim was only fifteen years old, riding the public bus home from a movie in downtown Hong Kong to his family's apartment in Stanley Village. The Schmidt family had lived in Hong Kong for nine years due to his dad's teaching position at the Hong Kong International School. Tim's arrest was the result of strict laws intended to identify and capture any illegal refugees who had entered Hong Kong from Viet Nam.

In 1979, the law required everyone to carry identification all of the time. Tim and his high school friend were without identification that night, so they were arrested and whisked off to the local jail. "As two Caucasians, we had no idea that the law was intended for us, too," they said. "Unfortunately, naïveté was not a welcome defense with the police officers."

When the boys called their homes, no one was there. "For three hours, it was a feeling of intense fear, isolation, and abandonment," Tim recalled. The kids' parents wouldn't learn of their plight until after 1 a.m. Eventually, both families were contacted, the boys' IDs were delivered to the jail, and both boys returned home to their families.

Looking back, these boys learned a penetrating life lesson. At a time in their lives when their independent interests were widening, they quickly became aware of their dependence on their families.

What Is Family?

Across society, we may debate the differences of faith and political or social backgrounds. However, we find little disagreement that the family is the natural and fundamental organizing unit of society. Not only do families reflect the strengths and weaknesses of our society as a whole, but they're also the primary agents of our sustainable development.

Yet the shape of that organizing unit has changed a lot recently. The *Leave It to Beaver* traditional family has become less common. There are more single-parent households, blended families, and same-sex households. And families without kids are on the rise. Perhaps the only clear definition of "family" is this: Every marriage creates a new family, but a marriage isn't required to create a family.

Our purpose of this chapter is less about identifying the types of families and more about spotlighting the critical role that family plays in our lives. Here's a quick summary of our research:

- Family was the only F to break into the high-satisfaction range of 8 plus.

- Family ranked number one in satisfaction across all participants, regardless of gender or age group.

- Family ranked number one as the highest priority for participants over the next three years.

- Family ranked as the F with the most people feeling qualified to mentor others.

Through personal interviews with families, we found common lessons on the value of weaving families together into tightly knit units. The common elements included having strong values and traditions, conveying a sense of belonging, sharing common experiences, communicating openly, planning time together, engaging multiple generations, and giving time and money freely to causes of the heart.

And spontaneity helps! During our professional women's focus group, one mother of two said, "Sometimes, it's the little things like taking the kids out for ice cream at 10 p.m. on a school night. They never forget it!"

A Continuous Work in Progress

One after another, our interviewees told us stories of dutiful ongoing commitments to ensure they are living up to their own expectations around family.

Vivek Agrawal, a partner with McKinsey & Company, modeled a strong family and parenting example to Tim one night after a long day of meetings. At exactly 7:25 p.m., Vivek told Tim, "I gotta go." After Tim inquired as to Agrawal's sudden urgency to depart, Agrawal said he needed to go home to read to his son and daughter.

Agrawal travels one to two days a week for his job, forty weeks a year, but he also works really hard to be a great dad. So, for example, whenever a new *Harry Potter* book comes out, he buys a copy, and every night when he is home, he and his kids read a chapter together.

Our conversation with Agrawal sparked his interest in doing even more with his family. "Now, I am going to work hard to read to my kids while I'm on the road, too, not allowing the miles in between us to steal my quality time with them."

Agrawal's son and daughter go to bed each night knowing their father cares enough to schedule and invest that time with them. That mindset is especially important when you consider how relatively quickly children enter and exit their parents' homes. Most kids are headed off to college or out of their parents' homes in just eighteen years—only about one-fourth of an average adult's lifespan!

Heidi and Earl Rogers don't take for granted a single moment of their kids' lives. After losing their son, Tate, at birth, they have dedicated their lives to blessing others who have experienced similar challenges.

"We have a home that is resilient," said Heidi, a business consultant and award-winning theater producer. She and Earl celebrate a family that is simultaneously intercultural, interracial, and blended. She is the daughter of white, Midwestern parents. Earl is half Native American and half African American and hails from the projects of St. Louis.

The Rogers's resiliency and openness to a variety of cultures has enabled them to open their home to a variety of newcomers. In addition to their own two biological children, Heidi and Earl have provided a welcome home environment to many other children.

> *"We make sure these kids understand that they are important to us . . . and our doors are always open."*

"We've always looked after kids who have been kicked out of their homes and would otherwise be homeless," Earl said. "We make sure these kids understand that they are important to us, they bring value to our home, and our doors are always open."

Tate would have been seven years old in 2010, but he is still an important part of the Rogers's family. Heidi and Earl's kindergartner asked his oldest blended sibling, "If you and Mom are white, my other brother and me are tan, and Dad is black, what color was Tate?" Out of the mouths of babes comes a significant lesson in family blending.

When we asked Chris Noonan to be a part of this book, he immediately asked about his wife, "Janet needs to be a part of this, too, right?" Noonan, executive vice president for AXA in Dallas, quickly identified the shared roles and responsibilities of parenthood in the Noonan household.

As parents of three children (ages fifteen, thirteen, and twelve), the Noonans have made family their prime focus. "We expect that we are each others' first priority," Janet said, with conviction. "It's one relationship you are born with, and it's one relationship you will die with."

In listening to the Noonans, it became clear they are very intentional in creating a strong family nucleus. "We live to set our kids free, [to encourage them] to be confident and successful, to find who they are, and to find a purpose and passion in life," Chris explained. The Noonans have a set of principles that serve as their anchor for their decision making and interactions.

The children each have their own "bucket list" of life goals. Chris asked, "What are you going to work toward in the next ninety days?"

Calendar meetings are critical. The Noonans take fifteen minutes every day to catch up and plan the near future. They pick and choose events to guard against over-busyness and encourage building the family unit.

> "We 'big-deal' birthdays."

Family vacations are vital. They create common experiences designed to last forever. Every Noonan family member plays a role in vacation preparation and engagement.

They celebrate one another. "We 'big-deal' birthdays," Chris said. "We celebrate that person by celebrating together."

Chris ended our visit with a comment that we came to see as a consistent theme among strong business leaders with extraordinarily strong families. He said, "I want and need the strength and confidence to perform at very high levels. And all of that support and success comes when my life is in balance—when my family is strong and vibrant. No amount of success is worth a failed family."

Other Types of Families

Family is not always about mom, dad, and the kids, however. Many professionals are living the life they imagined with mature, meaningful friendships that ultimately morph into family.

Consider the example of Shawn Moren, a human resources executive with SUPERVALU. As a teenager, Moren imagined a family with kids, but that's not how her life progressed. Instead, Moren has found family in a group of cherished friends. The time she invests with her core group of friends is more intentional than many others we interviewed with more traditional families.

"We have a group of single women friends who have become really important in my life," Moren explained. "We all work really hard, and we enjoy our work, but sometimes life is difficult. We drop what we are doing so we can be there for each other."

The closeness of Moren's friends became clear when one friend shared—in all seriousness—that she had been aggressively saving her money so that she could help take care of the others when they all quit working. "I was really impacted by her generosity," Moren said. "It's clear to me that she really does think of our group as her family. Why else would she make that sacrifice? Even though my life hasn't taken the shape I imagined when I was younger, I have a great sense of who I am, and I have a great family."

And let's not forget that many families today are created when children are born to single mothers without the intention of having a father around. Some families have two moms. And other families have two dads.

Paul learned a lot about healthy and unhealthy families as board chair of a powerful social services organization. After hearing pointed stories about family abuse that sent kids out onto the street, his mental picture of family changed significantly.

"More and more, I'm starting to think we need to worry less about the structure of the family and worry more that people are safe, loved, and well fed—both spiritually and nutritionally," Paul said. "Can you imagine how much better our world would be if everyone grew up and lived in a healthy family?"

Family Creativity

Sometimes, maintaining a strong family bond takes extraordinary creativity. "My husband and I made the deliberate decision to pursue vocations that were very important to the lives we imagined," said Jill Schumann. She and her husband met later in life and are happily married with no children.

A few years ago, Schumann was hired as CEO of LSS, one of the world's largest social service organizations. It was her dream job, but it meant that she and her husband would need to live in separate cities for more than ten years, based also on the responsibilities of his job. "We were determined to make sure the experience would strengthen our sense of family," she explained.

Through the challenge, the Schumanns intentionally developed three ways to stay connected. She explained: "We decided that we could pray at the same time every day. And whenever we could, we looked at the same sky together while talking on the phone. And we found it rewarding to listen to the same NPR programs, so we could discuss the same things. It was really important that we created specific things to share while we were apart. As we plan the next phase of our lives, we hope to be living in the same house, but we'll always remember how we maintained that strong sense of family while we lived apart."

What about the Sandwich Family?

With life expectancies increasing and people waiting until later in life to have children, more families are forced into the middle of a care-giving sandwich—when both children and parents are dependent on the care of middle-aged adults.

"The stress of watching our parents lose their ability to care for themselves or handle their own money has been really difficult," one woman explained. She was driving her youngest kids to and from middle school and high school and guiding her oldest child through college, but she was also monitoring the doctor visits and checkbook of her aging parents.

"It's tough for me to give myself a clean score on family," said one man we interviewed. He talked about giving himself a "9" on his nuclear family of five, but only a "2" on his extended family, commenting on the deteriorating health of his parents and their relationship with each other. "For a while, my parents were just not able to live in the same home together safely. That was really difficult for all of our family," he commented. "Thank heavens they are both on the mend and putting their lives back together." Today, his parents are back at home, living together, and taking care of each other.

Caution: Work Can Intrude

Compounding the difficulty of sandwich parenting is the demand of increasingly time-consuming work. "I think I'm a workaholic" was the all-too-common response we received as we interviewed leaders for this book. Many respondents shared that they feel like their mind is occupied with work about 90 percent of the time.

"Work is the first thing on my mind in the morning and the last thing on my mind in the evening when I hit the pillow," admitted one leader, who preferred to remain anonymous. Even Saturdays and Sundays were manipulated so that this leader could get in a few extra hours of work without his family feeling any negative effects.

Many leaders we met were yearning to be better moms, dads, husbands, wives, brothers, or sisters. However, they admitted that even during their designated family times, they were also making their business to-do lists, checking their digital assistants, or catching up on work on their laptops! No wonder Dan Mallin has a log-off policy at his family's cabin, as explained in more detail in Chapter 5.

To varying degrees, we are all consumed with this constant tug-of-war between our families and the rest of the world. However, when we lose the battle, it results in broken marriages, strained parent or sibling relationships, or children who feel marginalized.

One of the most present challenges is avoiding what one woman called, "chronic partial engagement." She worried that she was always thinking about too many things at once, effectively multitasking, but only going an inch deep on everything.

The danger of thinking like this is that we slowly and unconsciously begin to treat work and family relationships like the *CliffsNotes* version of a tantalizing novel. If you're a parent of young children, do you really want to treat them—even unintentionally—like an afterthought?

Family-raising behaviors like these were called the "microwave philosophy" by a leader we met. Unfortunately, through microwave parenting, the people we love the most end up being treated like reheated leftovers out of a shallow Styrofoam box. In . . . out . . . bell rings . . . done.

Family Bonds during Life's Trials

Many respondents spoke of how divorce put them in a place where they had an acute need for their extended family. At age thirty, Darcy Dilly-Cooper became a single mom with three kids, ages seven, six, and three. "It was really tough," she said, "trying to balance the role of working mom and at-home mom. It creates enormous stress on the family unit."

During these times, Dilly-Cooper, an executive in the franchise industry, leaned on the wisdom of her father. Although he had passed away just prior to her divorce, she kept in mind his attitude of perseverance and fortitude through adversity.

"He was always teaching us life lessons," Dilly-Cooper reflected. "From his German heritage, I can still hear him saying, 'If you want something, life won't hand it to you. You must work hard.'"

Since then, Dilly-Cooper remarried, and her children are now wonderful adults. When we spoke with her, she and her husband, Harris, and their children had just returned from a bucket-list trip to Israel. "It was incredible to have such amazing family togetherness amidst that huge faith experience," she shared.

These Are Role Models?

Despite the high degree of satisfaction with family, doesn't it seem like it's getting tougher to find positive public role models for our family members to emulate? For instance, 2009 seemed to be a veritable who's who year of moral hypocrisy as we witnessed the public breakdown of family values among such prestigious leaders as former New York Governor Eliot Spitzer, former presidential candidate John Edwards, South Carolina Governor Mark Sanford, and golfing champion Tiger Woods.

Woods's fall from grace was the most mind-bending. He had unprecedented talent, seemingly limitless wealth, and worldwide recognition and respect—and lest we forget, a beautiful wife and two healthy kids. We were all shocked when we saw his Cadillac SUV wrapped around a tree. But we were even more appalled when we learned of his woman-in-every-town lifestyle. With that meteoric fall from grace, it's not surprising we've seen him struggling on the golf course since then.

The common connection among these leaders is that we expected values-centric leadership and moral judgment from them. Instead, what we got was a bunch of people in power winding up in scandals that wrecked their families. How could this be? Joe Magee of New York University's Wagner Graduate School of Public Service commented, "In their minds, they're not being brazen. They forget there are rules governing what they do. They're just pursuing their own desires."

Jay's Success Story

But not all powerful people go awry. Jay, who was mentioned in the introduction, is an internationally acclaimed retina surgeon with an MD in ophthalmology and a PhD in biomedical engineering from Seoul, South Korea. Jay was a workaholic who showed interest in adopting the Seven Fs model after meeting Tim on an international flight.

Tim was elated to discover that the Seven Fs had created some lasting changes in Jay particularly around family. "Several months after we originally met, Jay shared that he was so moved by our conversation that he was making significant progress in specific areas that needed attention," Tim said. "A year later, he is now married and lost a lot of weight. As a result, his original low scores on family [5] and fitness [3] have skyrocketed. It was a blast to see Jay internalize the Seven Fs and intentionally make significant progress on his life."

The more we researched the Seven Fs, and the more we heard the success stories of others, the more we became convinced that people—even workaholics—could positively change their lives based on receiving new and compelling information about a better way.

Kiss and Tell

The *Wall Street Journal* in February 2010 featured an article titled "Happy Couples Kiss and Tell." This article featured couples who had been married for forty, fifty, or even more than sixty years and what we might glean from their decades of conjugal bliss. As reporter Elizabeth Bernstein wrote, "In other words, they beat the odds [of divorce]. It is often possible to understand why a marriage fails, as so many do. It is much more difficult though to elucidate why one succeeds. Why do some couples thrive, while others fizzle or flame out, despite their best intentions?"

Some of the couples who were interviewed were President Jimmy and Rosalynn Carter (sixty-three years), Rocker Ozzy and Sharon Osbourne (twenty-eight years), and poker star Doyle and Louise Brunson (forty-eight years).

Common themes in the "do" column among the couples were have your own work and your own projects; forgive; compromise; include a combination of hard work and sheer blind luck; find the middle ground; embrace humor; never, ever give up; and stay alive.

Bernstein concluded, "My sister, a doctor, told me about one of her patients, a ninety-two-year-old woman who showed up for her appointment with her husband, who was ninety-four. They said they had been married for almost seventy years. My sister, highly impressed, asked the couple the secret to their union's longevity. And they looked at each other for a long moment. Then the wife spoke, 'Eh, neither of us died.'"

SUCCESS HABIT: Family

"Looking back, the one thing that was wonderful for me was 'Daddy-Daughter Date Night.' When I was in junior high, my dad took me out on dates where we could just spend time together and talk. I intend to make sure my husband does that with our daughters—hopefully someday."

SUCCESS HABIT: Family

"A few years ago, I took a cue about my family health from the people who suggest treating savings as mandatory for my financial health. Now I block out time on my calendar on Thursdays to spend time with my grandson. Nobody messes with my Thursday afternoons!"

SUCCESS HABIT: Family

"I contact my aging parents almost every other day, and I try to visit them every other week. I try to listen to my inner voice when they tell me I don't need to come over and check on them. Its hard stepping over that line of them being parents and me being responsible for them."

Seven Fs

3

Faith

Family

Finances

Fitness

Friends

Fun

Future

Discussing finances is very personal. There are many ways to discuss the other Fs at a dinner party, but we stop short of asking, "How happy are you with your finances?" Even if we did, we'd dance around the subject, because it's not polite to ask other people about their money.

It's a little odd, because our spending habits are highly visible, but the balance in our checkbook is very private. A bold pastor we interviewed hit the nail on the head about why people are so reticent about their finances: "You give me five minutes in anyone's checkbook, and I'll show you their values!"

In general, we think that's a good thing. However, Paul's not really sure he wants any of us to know how much money he really spends tinkering with his golf game! Case in point: most of the people interviewed for this chapter were happy to share their stories about their finances, but they preferred not to be mentioned by name.

Through our research, we uncovered three components about finances that deserve illumination:

1. Making intentional, early choices regarding finances

2. Developing a personal understanding of how much we *really need* (instead of what we *think* we need)

3. Having thankful attitudes

When those three conditions are present, you actually can *buy happiness*.

Like physical health, financially healthy choices often require uncomfortable discipline. For instance, we all know we should exercise and we all know we should save money. And yet, we have finely tuned expectations about how we want to live right now. For many, that vision creates a payment-to-payment routine.

As long as incomes are steady, this cycle works. But what happens when the payment promises exceed the income?

Forced to Make Choices

"I didn't see it coming," one professional woman explained about the loss of her job. "We knew business was bad, but I was working harder than ever and I'd always gotten good performance reviews. When I heard the words 'laid off,' I was totally in shock."

Stories of professional people losing their jobs are more common nowadays, but this story has a very important message about handling your finances in lieu of adverse circumstances. As she relayed, "We sat down and really examined our lives and our spending. Within an hour, we cut hundreds of dollars a month in spending on stuff that wasn't all that important. We used my severance and some of our savings to pay off some loan balances."

She continued, "What a huge relief! Just two months after losing my job, my husband and I were feeling very grateful. Today, we still have money to take our summer vacation and we have more time to enjoy our kids. We are feeling much less pressure, and the past two years have been much, much happier."

The Research

The majority of those who took the Seven Fs survey are middle to upper-income people: college-educated people, salaried workers, or business owners. Here's a quick look at what we learned:

- Two-thirds of respondents claimed they were making as much or more money than they expected at this point in their lives.

- Finances ranked next-to-last in satisfaction—just before Fitness.

- Finances was the second-most difficult F to live up to one's own expectations (again, just before Fitness).

As a reality check, one obvious thing needs to be stated: It's reasonable to surmise that those who live near the poverty line may think and feel differently about their finances than the Seven Fs survey people. Anyone who is struggling to provide basic food, shelter, and safety has a different motivation than saving.

All the more reason to ponder this fact: Even though most of us are making as much or more money than we expected and financial satisfaction is difficult to achieve, is it possible we don't know how much is enough?

Planning Ahead Helps

"I gave myself a '9' on finances because I know exactly how much cash flow we need to live without worrying about money," one of our interviewees explained. He's a consultant who has survived two separate economic slowdowns. "Years ago, when we were first married, my wife and I decided we should learn to live on only one income, even though we were both working. We also decided to be well-insured. That turned out to be really important for us, because we've been battling my wife's illness for five years now. Who knows how much longer we will have together? We feel very grateful today. Without our savings and insurance, we'd spend a lot of energy worrying about money."

Interesting—two different interviews, two entirely different financial situations, and yet both interviewees used the term "grateful" to describe their financial situation. Could "gratitude" help explain people's positive attitudes about their finances?

Jean Chatsky, a celebrity financial reporter, and Robert Emmons, a professor of psychology at the University of California–Davis, agree that being grateful is a central concept to financial satisfaction. Emmons has dedicated his career to studying gratitude. He outlines three significant benefits for increasing our financial satisfaction when learning to practice gratitude:

1. Having daily grateful thoughts had been shown to increase personal happiness levels by as much as 25 percent.

2. Journaling about gratefulness just a few minutes a day over three weeks showed lasting positive effects for six months.

3. Cultivating gratitude had positive effects on general health—most specifically better sleep

"Gratitude is literally one of the few things that can measurably change people's lives," explained Emmons in his book, *Thanks: How the New Science of Gratitude Can Make You Happier.*

He writes: "Gratitude is a quality that we should aspire to as part and parcel of personal growth, but first, we have to overcome an innate human 'negativity bias.'" His research confirms that even when we are not feeling stressed, we are naturally inclined to think negatively about our financial condition. So when things in our lives become more difficult, we are prone to be increasingly more negative about money.

Chatsky agrees. She told a *Reader's Digest* reporter, "I have been working in the trenches with real people and their real money for close to two decades." Her book *The*

Difference is specifically about how to feel successful, even in the most difficult financial times. Her research included the study of 5,000 households between 2008–2009. In nine chapters of advice, she lands on gratitude as the key concept that wraps the other eight chapters together.

Learning Financial Literacy

So what does it take to be grateful for what you have and in turn achieve a sense of financial contentment?

A fifty-something partner in a professional services firm was totally fixated on getting to $3 million for retirement. He described himself as "trapped in a white collar job that I've hated for more than five years now." He thought he needed $3 million in retirement savings to match the cash flow from his current income.

At age fifty-six, he hired his first financial planner, who encouraged him to calm down. With careful planning and conservative investing, he saw that a much smaller number could provide the lifestyle he wanted, and he could cut back his job to half-time. "It was the slap in the face that I needed," he said. "I was racing toward my number, and I was becoming exhausted physically and emotionally. Turns out, my number was within my reach."

One octogenarian we interviewed lived through both the 1931 and 2008 stock market crises. Factually, the 50 percent drop in the 2008 S&P 500 was nearly identical to the drop in 1931. Seventy-nine years later, his hardship wasn't the same, but his urge to hunker down and save was still alive. His father died during the Great Depression, and he was needed as the man of the house ever since. Even though he has plenty of money today, every spending decision in his life was shaped by the experience of caring for his mother and sisters.

Contrast that gentleman's upbringing with the attitude of many kids today. With many people from today's generation, HDTV, cell phones, Facebook, and retail therapy are viewed as birthrights. It's understandable, because kids see their parents spending on those "needed" things. In moments of weakness, any of us can start to believe that we need such things to make us happy and content.

Financial attitudes like these make the work of people like Nathan Dungan even more important. Dungan is the founder and president of Share Save Spend, a consultancy whose mission is to help youth and adults achieve "financial sanity," as he calls it. His firm provides books, tools, and inspirational programs to help parents, schools, corporations, churches, and communities educate individuals and families about the intersection of their values and money.

Dungan left a prosperous career as a financial advisor and marketing executive for a *Fortune* 500 firm to help people learn how to develop and maintain healthy money habits. He speaks and writes with authority about how children form both positive and negative financial habits from living within the influence of their family norms.

> *For many families, money is a very personal, private subject—even more so than sex.*

For many families, money is a very personal, private subject—even more so than sex. So, kids are forced to learn by observation. "Money is the 8,000-pound elephant in the living room," Dungan said. "Because so many families struggle to communicate effectively about money, it can lead to enormous amounts of misunderstanding, confusion, and unhealthy behavior."

What are kids learning on their own today? According to Share Save Spend:

- American households with credit card debt have seen the average total balance swell to nearly $16,000.

- The 28 million teens in the United States spend $70 billion a year on food, gas, electronics, movies, and music.

- College students graduate with an average of four credit cards, $4,000 of credit card debt, and $26,000 of student loan debt.

Dungan and his colleagues espouse the virtue of teaching families about financial literacy, through the concepts of sharing, saving, and spending—in that order. Sharing cultivates the spirit of gratitude, because it helps us think about others who are less fortunate. Saving is about establishing healthy habits of investing in one's own future. Spending is what we use to live. "Research has shown that when people focus less on spending, and more on sharing and saving, they are happier, healthier, and wealthier," Dungan said.

Can We Find the Joy in Money?

"We think the key to living well is to try to get people to focus on joy management, instead of wealth management," explained Brad Hewitt, CEO of Thrivent Financial for Lutherans, a *Fortune* 500 social enterprise that invests its profits back into its communities by virtue of being a tax-exempt financial services company.

"I think we've all let Wall Street persuade us into thinking that we should focus on getting as much as we can by way of return on investment of our money," Hewitt said. "Of course it's important to have a healthy return on investments. But in our experience, watching your money grow doesn't increase happiness or decrease fear. The happiest people are those who are thinking about 'who can I serve with my money that brings me the most joy?'"

Hewitt, the son of parents who lived during the Great Depression, learned their thrifty habits and initially found it difficult to adopt the values of giving to others. "At first it was scary, and I think it is scary for a lot of people who worry that they won't have enough," he said. "We know a wealthy person who was miserly and very worried about saving enough. It became an obsession where he couldn't even enjoy spending money on himself, his family, or others. His thriftiness made his life very difficult to enjoy, and that's sad."

Hewitt and his family have learned to live a joyous, generous life at home and at work. Through programs like Thrivent Builds with Habitat for Humanity and a local chapter system, the company is putting its money where its heart is. All Thrivent members have the opportunity to help themselves and others through volunteering, social activities, and local giving programs. "One of the greatest joys in our lives is seeing how much good we can accomplish through the giving of our members," Hewitt said. "It's a wonderful example of both personal and professional generosity that inspires us to give more and more each year."

Darrell and Norma Williams tried a radical thriftiness experiment in their lives and in the process found new joy. Darrell was a middle school teacher for more than thirty years, and Norma worked as a business manager. Together, they raised two daughters and welcomed their first grandchild. In their empty-nesting years, they pushed back against their consumer instincts and won. For the entire calendar year of 2008, they deliberately avoided purchasing anything new, except for food and fuel.

"It wasn't all that difficult," Darrell explained. "Except for when I really needed shoe strings for my favorite shoes—my first instinct was to go out and buy a new pair. But we found gently used shoe strings without too much trouble." Norma added, "It should be noted that we did stock up on toilet paper."

Surprisingly, the couple didn't rush out to the mall the day their experiment ended. "What we learned is that we have so many things in our lives that we truly value that don't require spending money," Norma said. "We haven't totally cut out shopping in our lives today, but we do spend a lot less, and give more. It feels great, and it makes me less worried about whether we will have 'enough' for our future."

The Family Cash Flow Spreadsheet

Learning how much is enough can have a profound effect on your psyche. For example, let's look at the story of a very successful female executive who received executive coaching from Paul.

"My biggest worry is that my kids will think that their happiness and success are correlated directly with money," the executive said. "I'm very fortunate. I've had a great career. I've made a lot of money, and my kids live a very privileged life, especially compared to how I grew up. However, it's not the money that's made me feel successful and happy. I wasn't happy until I took personal accountability to ask the question, 'Why don't I feel successful?'"

Thus, she and her husband sat down to look at their lives "like a spreadsheet, a family cash flow analysis," she said. "First, we looked at our obligations like the mortgages and other payments, and our college commitments. That was a big number! But then we looked at our 401(k), stock options, portfolio balance, and personal savings, and how much earning power we had. I was embarrassed when I saw on paper that I could have slowed down years ago. We have way, way more than we need."

> *"Our happiness multiplied when my husband and I started taking all of our vacation days."*

"Our happiness multiplied when my husband and I started taking all of our vacation days," she shared, "and when we started giving more to the church and taking volunteer vacations in developing third world countries. We started involving our kids in decisions about what charities to include in our philanthropy. The answer for me was this: I didn't know how much was enough.

The Big Questions

Eventually we all deal with the questions: "Will I have enough?" and "How much is enough?" The only real answer is that it depends. It depends on how much money we save, how long we can continue to earn an income, and how long we actually live.

Paul's grandmother, Arlene Hunter, lived a healthy, active life in her own home until she was 103 years old. Arlene's husband, Willis Kenneth Hunter, died of Parkinson's disease when she was in her early eighties. His nursing home care drained most of their savings. However, she remained vital and generous for twenty more years! How would she have possibly answered these questions when she was in her forties: "Will I have enough?" and "How much is enough?"

Now, with expanded life expectancies, it seems more difficult to have anything left.

That's a big concern for the Great Depression generation for whom leaving money behind for loved ones was once a huge motivator. They were taught to work really hard and save their money so they could retire comfortably and leave a nest egg for their children. Now, with expanded life expectancies, it seems more difficult to have anything left.

A couple in their eighties told us they were happy and living how they had imagined. He was in great shape and played golf two to three times a week. They had a summer home "up north" and a winter place "down south." But aging started to cost significant money. The wife had Alzheimer's disease. As full-time professional care neared, they lived in the fear of draining their life savings very quickly. It's a significant dilemma; they wanted the very best care, but they didn't want to be a financial burden for their children.

So, that leaves baby boomers thinking more about what kind of work they can enjoy for the rest of their lives. Just as with Paul's grandmother, even small amounts of income can help ease the financial pressure late into life, especially if it's something joyful. One woman explained, "I'm way past when I thought I would quit working. I don't think about retirement. I love my work. Why not work? I'm making some money to stretch my life's savings, and I'm still having fun!"

Getting Ahead

Wherever you are, whatever your age, it takes money to live. And the standard of living we expect has a significant effect on how much pressure we feel around our finances. But unless we win the lottery, or hit it big with a risky start-up, the only other way to build a nest egg is to spend less than we make.

Tim is a huge fan of the *Millionaire Next Door* philosophy, the best-seller that showed that people who had success with their finances made really good decisions along the way about what not to spend money on. The people profiled in the book bought used cars, wore Timex watches, and cut coupons. They were frugal with the everyday things, so they could spend generously on the things that were really important to them.

"That message really rings true with me," Tim said. "My parents were missionaries, and for several years our family lived in Hong Kong. We were very happy with very little money. After college, I started my career as a school teacher and coach on $12,000 a year. Jeanette and I learned how to live on very little money, and we still have the same mentality today. We share 10 percent, we save 20 percent, and live on the remaining 70 percent. So far, that's really worked for us."

Based on the successes shared by so many of our interviewees about their finances, we believe you have the power to buy your own happiness by determining your financial direction, understanding how much you need, and being grateful for what you have. What's the first move for you?

SUCCESS HABIT: Finances

"Once a week, after the kids are in bed, my husband and I go through all of the previous week's bills and our future spending requests. Because we started it a couple of years ago, we have greatly reduced our anxiety over money, and we're having more fun."

SUCCESS HABIT: Finances

"My wife and I always discuss any purchase that is more than $250. Early in our marriage that amount was $50; as the years have gone by, we've gradually increased that amount. It helps us keep an open conversation about money, and it keeps us communicating about things that are important to each of us."

SUCCESS HABIT: Finances

"My dad taught me to set up an automatic payment from my paycheck every two weeks into a money market savings account that serves as my safety money. It's really helped with car repairs and all the travel I've had to do for my college friends' weddings. And there is still a lot of money in there . . . thanks Dad!"

Seven Fs

4

Faith

Family

Finances

Fitness

Friends

Fun

Future

> *"A man's health can be judged by which he takes two at a time: pills or stairs."*

–Joan Welsh

No matter your current fitness status, you can likely recount the euphoric high you experienced from some vigorous physical activity, like an early-morning walk or run, followed by a full day of nutritional eating. How often, however, do we finish off a winning fitness day with something that undermines our prior efforts, like a warm, double fudge brownie and ice cream at around 9:30 p.m.?

Or perhaps you've felt the adrenaline rush of an intense workout regimen, followed by a meeting in which you've been completely "on," only to end the day with a "dinner" of margaritas, guacamole, and chips during happy hour.

Or maybe you've experienced the absolute conviction on New Year's Day to change—to finally lose weight and get fit, to attend a heart-pumping aerobics or Pilates class five days a week and fit into that new dress or bathing suit for the summer—only to hit the snooze button three times on January 8th and barely drag your "love handles" or "muffin tops" into work.

Pills or Stairs?

We end up "shoulding" all over ourselves. "I really should lose fifteen pounds." "I should order that salad." "I should drink more water." But we don't. Why not?

Fitness, our research confirmed, is the "throwaway F":

- It ranked lowest in satisfaction (87.9 percent said "low" to "moderate" satisfaction).

- It ranked the most difficult of the Seven Fs to live up to our expectations.

- It ranked fourth on our three-year priority list.

- It ranked last in importance in terms of "living the life I imagine."

In a nutshell, the vast majority of our survey respondents said, "I'm not happy with my fitness. It's hard, and I'm really not going to do much about it!" We were told that because fitness is so challenging to work into daily routines, it gets pushed aside, in favor of doubling down on the other Fs. Thus, we dubbed fitness as the throwaway F.

This was a challenging insight, because the other Fs depend, frankly, on having at least a minimum level of fitness and health. As it's been said many times, including in the movie *The Princess Bride*, "If you haven't got your health, then you haven't got anything."

In our research for this chapter, we sought to find people who had successfully blended a fitness rhythm into their lives without it becoming a daily roller coaster of ups and downs. We sought people who had high energy, vitality, and good health, without the mountain tops and deep valleys of inconsistency.

We interviewed many leaders who have had long-term, consistent fitness success and have built a virtual barbwire fence around themselves to protect against the evils of colossal portions, empty nutrition, and couch potato fitness—in short, people whose fitness enables and compels them to lead exceptional lives.

Worldly Fitness Education

Several years ago, a young but daring guy from Minnesota contacted the Guinness Book of World Records and asked, "If I biked from the upper Midwest to Argentina, would that be a world record?"

The record authorities said, "No. But if you biked from Prudhoe Bay, Alaska, the northern extreme of North America, to the southern extreme of South America, we would consider it."

He said, "Okay." And after a year of fund-raising, in 1986, Dan Buettner and his brother Steve conquered the Americas by bike. Ten months, five days, and fourteen hours later, they had cycled 15,500 miles and set a world record.

Since then, Buettner has become an internationally-known fitness expert and *New York Times* best-selling author who has appeared on *Oprah*, *Dr. Oz*, *CNN's Anderson Cooper*, and *Fox News*. Most recently, he published a book, *The Blue Zones: Lessons for Living Longer from the People Who Have Lived the Longest*.

Buettner's book is a first-hand look at the cultures around the world, dubbed "Blue Zones," in which people's embedded living habits have contributed to lifespans ten to twelve years longer, on average, than in the United States. He identified what these communities have in common and distilled their secrets into nine lifestyle habits.

We asked Buettner the focal question: "How does having this knowledge of the Blue Zones directly manifest itself in your day-to-day life? What really works to keep you fit?"

Set Your Life up Right

"The bottom line," Buettner said, "is to set your life up right and design your life in such a way that you are naturally active." He continued, "Exercise [for the sake of exercise] is the wrong strategy. Blue Zone people don't pump iron."

Personally practicing what he preaches, the day we met, Buettner rode his bike to work (four miles) then biked to our meeting (about a mile away). In all, he would bike about ten miles, which for him was an average day of riding.

The prior day, Buettner had several conference calls, so he grabbed his telephone headset and began walking around a nearby lake. "It's all in how you design your life," he explained.

"We're also hard-wired to consume calories," Buettner said. "We can't escape the cultural trifecta of sugar, fat, and salt." Even clichés like, "bring home the bacon" and "he's a meat and potatoes guy" connect masculine qualities such as virility and strength with the consumption of meat.

When setting up our lunch, Buettner suggested a natural, organic restaurant. There was no temptation for a burger and fries because they weren't on the menu. Instead, our lunch was a cacophony of color, nutrition, and natural and local foods to a bounty of salmon, vegetables, and spices.

Other tools and sound bites from Buettner:

- Walking is the only way to stave off cognitive decline into your hundreds. A brisk forty-five-minute walk every day is all you need.

- Perform exercises that support your basic muscle strength and sense of balance. As we age, joint health and bone mass become important. Poor balance and falling often negatively affect longevity.

- The more meat you eat, the quicker you die! Epidemiological studies followed millions of people for a decade to confirm: go easy on the meat. Centenarians in Buettner's study had primarily a plant-based diet, with meats saved for special occasions.

- Twenty-five percent of our life expectancy is in our genes; 75 percent is in our lifestyles. Which can you control?

After spending time with Buettner and allowing his bottom-line directive—set your life up right—to marinate, Tim found himself directly affected by Buettner's counsel while shopping at a Saturday morning flea market near his cabin. Tim's big purchase? An antique 18" Craftsman reel lawn mower for $25—completely human propelled and a heck of a workout!

That weekend, Tim's double-blade John Deere gas-powered tractor created no noise or pollution as Tim took his "new" mower for a spin around the yard. He loved the experience of getting his heart pumping and sweat dripping off his brow, just like the centenarians in the Blue Zones!

Faked Fitness

Today, we are spending billions trying to create the illusion of fitness. Freedonia Group, a market research firm based in Cleveland, determined that by 2008, products promising to make people look and feel young had become a booming $28 billion-a-year US industry. In fact, we may even be spending more time and money on the illusion of fitness than on actually getting fit. Expensive clothes, Spandex, cosmetics, high heels, padded shoulders, and even sports cars help us artificially send messages of health, wealth, and wisdom to our brains.

And in the end, seldom is anyone fooled into thinking we are suddenly fit.

Investing a lot of time and energy in makeup and expensive clothes to mask an unhealthy, out-of-shape physical self is unlikely to make you satisfied or confident. And it can keep you from investing the time, money, and energy in developing the real health and fitness you'd prefer to enjoy.

Authentic Fitness

"You can have all the rest" was the gut punch delivered to Meghan Huber at the start of sixth-grade recess. Each captain for the kickball game took turns choosing which kids they wanted on their team until only a motley crew remained.

This shameful image was burned into the mind of Meghan Huber, one of the shorter classmates being dismissed by her peers. Her self-talk became, "I'm not an athlete. I'll never stack up in sports. My peers are all better than me. I am the 'arm' in Red Rover that everyone wants to run through."

She knew she needed to be in better shape to do her job well.

This self-talk stayed with Huber for more than thirty years. She never pursued any sports in high school or college. But as an adult, working long hours as a large project construction manager, she knew she needed to be in better shape to do her job well. "I was an off-again, on-again exerciser," she shared.

71

Then, something changed. Huber began attending marathon races to support her husband and saw the people who were coming in two hours after the leaders had finished. "I began to see myself among that [later-finishing] crowd," Huber admitted.

The high-fives, encouragement, and exuberance among the slower-paced runners and their supporters planted a seed in Huber's mind. *I can do this!* she enthusiastically thought. And soon, she began to run marathons herself.

Out of that enthusiasm and passion, Huber started the annual Women Run the Cities road race in 2007 in Minneapolis, which now attracts more than 2,500 female runners each year. She makes the race challenging, yet "uniquely feminine." Women can race with their girlfriends and run in a safe, judgment-free environment.

For Huber, the value of running is simply participating, not timing herself. "When I run marathons, I'm still at the back. I have to check to see if the race closes on five-hour marathoners like me," Huber said. "My husband will finish in three hours, go home, shower, have lunch, and come back to see me finish. I run slow . . . but I run!"

Other insights from Huber:

- **Commit:** When exercising, make the commitment to yourself: "I have to show up! I even ran in the rain this morning."

- **Create:** "If I run, I know I am going to have a better day. I make that deposit in my 'fitness and creativity account,' and the energy rush pays me back all day."

- **Inspire:** "Running has created an alter-ego from my kickball days—confidence, inspiration, insight into myself, and the ability to deal with stress."

- **Resolve:** "It's okay to be the person to bring up the rear. Do something with purpose."

Paul Hillen stepped on the scale and was aghast. He hadn't weighed himself in a number of years. His internal voice said, "I'm probably in the 230 range, which is about okay for someone six feet tall." When 265 pounds leapt off Hillen's digital scale, he agonized over the thought, "I am closer to 300 pounds than I am to 200!" At that moment, he started his journey to turn his life around and get fit.

Today, Hillen is 180 pounds—and holding.

"I had a complete lifestyle change," explained Hillen, a vice president with Cargill, the food and agricultural conglomerate. He made three significant life changes that remain constant today. Each day, he drinks one hundred ounces of water and exercises every morning on an elliptical trainer while watching the news. He also reduced his calories by about half. "My suit size went from fifty-one to forty-two, my waist shrunk from forty-four to thirty-two inches, and my resting heart rate reduced from sixty-seven to forty-two beats per minute," he said. "My energy has gone through the roof."

Other Hillen insights:

- **Track:** Count your calories every day.

- **Monitor:** Weigh in every morning.

- **Strive:** Don't let your fitness regimen keep you from having fun.

73

Pursuing Code RED

We want to look good, feel good, live healthier, and live longer. However, we have a fitness epidemic on our hands. With more than 1 billion overweight adults in the world, according to the World Health Organization, there have never been so many "human mastodons" striding the earth as there are now.

In an era of obesity and sedentary living, maintaining a fit and healthy body requires what we've dubbed "Code RED": reduction, education, and discipline. As our survey research mounted, these three themes kept emerging as definitive success factors to fitness.

For example, a recent major study provided one recipe for cutting your risk of diabetes, heart attack, stroke, or cancer by 78 percent. The recipe? Avoid smoking, exercise three to four days per week; maintain a body mass index less than thirty; and eat a diet favoring fruits, vegetables, and whole grains. That sounds pretty convincing to us!

Reduction

In Okinawa, Japan, people often begin a meal with the adage, *"Hara hachi bu,"* which is essentially a reminder to stop eating when their stomachs are 80 percent full. In the United States, which easily leads the world in obesity, we eat until we are completely full. Portion control appears to be a major problem, as the 2004 movie about fast-food overconsumption, *Super Size Me*, demonstrated in spades.

One of the Travel Channel's most popular programs is *Man vs. Food*, in which the host visits restaurants around the country to eat gargantuan meals, like an eleven-pound pizza or a twelve-pound hamburger. For the sake of the host's future health, we hope he also mixes in a salad or workout when he's off-camera.

Even the famous Leonardo da Vinci painting, "The Last Supper," has seen its reproductions super sized over the last 1,000 years. A food and brand laboratory at Cornell University took the fifty-two most famous paintings of the Last Supper over the past ten centuries and compared the head sizes of Christ's disciples to the sizes of the plates, entrees, and loaves of bread. The study, published in the *International Journal of Obesity*, found that the meals had grown by 69 percent and plate sizes had grown by 66 percent.

> *Even regular restaurant meals now seem to come in only one size: extra-large.*

Even regular restaurant meals now seem to come in only one size: extra-large. "My husband and I have been splitting restaurant entrees for over a year now," said one professional speaker in her forties, "and I'm still stunned by how much food we get."

To help feel more full when dining, the couple also frequently asks for a carafe of water with their shared meal. "These two reduction habits shaved hundreds of empty calories from our waistlines," she said.

Education

By increasing your knowledge and awareness of nutrition, exercise, and portion control, you are far more likely to make the right health choices. Nutrition and wellness books like *Blue Zones* or *Body for Life* lay out proven habits for fitness success. Even the magazines *Men's Health* or *Women's Health*, or television's *The Biggest Loser* (now seen in twenty-three countries), can provide valuable insights for achieving the fit life we imagine.

Education is often the key to adopting a healthier and more productive life. For example, did you know that recent research has shown that prolonged periods of stress—as revealed by stress hormones measured in your hair—can be a more accurate predictor of a heart attack than high blood pressure, high cholesterol, or smoking? Or did you know that drinking two eight-ounce glasses of water before every breakfast, lunch, and dinner is a proven weight-loss habit, according to researchers at Virginia Tech? Water fuels weight loss and prolonged good health.

Discipline

Discipline is the most important habit of all, and it rests on your own shoulders. Gone are the days of childhood, when you could count on a parent or well-meaning adult to steer you in the right fitness direction. Instead, as adults, we need to take responsibility for our own well being, commit to it, and follow through on ways to achieve it. A personal trainer we interviewed said that 85 percent of weight loss and fitness is what you choose to stick in your mouth every day. That includes consumption of alcohol and tobacco.

We believe goal-setting is one of the greatest disciplines for becoming and remaining fit. Paul admitted, "I hate exercise. I can think of any reason not to do it . . . until I have a goal!"

Paul has a consistent goal that drives his fitness and discipline: Stay mentally and physically fit enough to shoot his age in golf. "Sure, I want to stay healthy, so I can be a good husband, father, and friend . . . but it's the golf goal that motivates me," he said. Recently, Paul walked one hundred holes of golf—thirty-eight miles over fourteen hours straight—for a charity event. Preparing for the event inspired him to complete one hundred thirty-minute workouts to get in shape. "I was in the best shape of my adult life," he said.

"Always having a goal is paramount," said Ed Deutschlander, co-president of North Star Resource Group. "My workouts are all scheduled on my calendar weeks in advance, so I am certain to get them in."

Deutschlander is a fit, five-foot-ten, 185-pound forty-year-old and father of four active kids. He wanted to be crystal-clear with us that setting fitness goals is key to his long-term fitness triumph. "I ran five miles this morning," he said. "Why? Because I'm signed up for a race with my sisters in two weeks. If that race wasn't on the calendar, I never would have run this morning. And after that race, I'll set another goal."

Set your fitness goal today, and begin moving toward the fit life you imagine.

During our interviews for this book, we observed a number of clever success habits that helped other fit leaders overcome their own fitness fallibilities. See if any of these might be helpful to you:

- **The Shoe Swap:** Three buddies take each others' shoes home from the gym every day. That way, they are 100 percent accountable to each other to show up, so that the other guy can work out with his own shoes.

- **Fatbet.net:** This is an electronic accountability website used by some of our survey respondents. You assemble a team of individuals who seek to lose weight, with each participant wagering they'll each lose a certain number of pounds by a specific date. Every week, an automatic reminder and visual graph of each dieter's progress shows up via email. Those who achieve their weight loss goals win; those who don't must pay up on their Fatbet wager. "The machismo and ribbing in the message board was very motivating," said one competitor.

- **Two Alarm Clocks:** A sales executive set his alarm clock for 5:00 a.m. each day and placed another alarm clock set for 5:01 in his sleeping three-month-old's nursery. The motivation, of course, was to get up and race to the infant's room before the second alarm clock rang. As he shared, "Once I was up, I worked out. Otherwise I'd hit the snooze button."

Combining Family and Fitness

Joseph Otting, a banking executive in Los Angeles, had an extreme job that included 60 percent travel over the last year, visiting nearly every metro area in the United States. With his rigorous schedule as CEO of OneWest Bank, it would be understandable if he were overweight and unfit. However, Otting, at age fifty-two, was a model of physical fitness: six-foot-one and 175 pounds. He thanked his parents for these positive fitness examples they modeled:

- **Be active:** Otting observed his mom taking time to walk or swim four to five times per week, while his dad played golf or tennis for the physical and social advantages.

- **Eat well:** Meals were always healthy and well-balanced.

- **Include thoughtful meals:** Dinner was expected to be shared as a family. Healthy food and good communication kept Otting's family fit and connected.

But it wasn't just his parents' examples that led Otting to the fitness success he had achieved. The impetus was based on his typical ninety-minute workday commute in L.A. gridlock. Otting was essentially trapped in his car for three hours every day. But twenty-six years ago, he learned that if he left his house at 5 a.m., his commute time was cut to forty minutes total.

And there began Otting's fitness regimen of getting out of the house before rush hour and spending those formerly lost ninety minutes working out near his office. Running, biking, swimming, and weights kept it fresh and varied.

In the spirit of *What Really Works*, we asked Otting, "What was your workout today?" He said, "I biked twenty-five minutes, did weights for twenty-five minutes, and read the paper in the steam room.

Other insights from Otting:

- Pick hotels based on their gyms. You will work out more consistently.

- When traveling, pack your gym clothes first and put them next to the TV. Visual cues work.

- Keep your workouts interesting. Add kayaking, mountain climbing, or biking.

- Be willing to go to a personal trainer. Learn something new. Ask for help, and get involved in an exercise group for accountability.

Climbing Your Mountain

In his own attempt to blend fitness and family, Tim climbed Washington's Mt. Rainier in 2010 with his twenty-one-year-old son, Jon. "Having a goal to climb to 14,400 feet on a glacier certainly created a Code RED opportunity for me," Tim explained. Half of Tim's challenge was simply preparing for his climb. "A reduction in nutritionless, harmful calories helped me tone up and lose twenty-five pounds—half the weight of my backpack. Plus my internal desire to keep up with my son created the discipline to stay on course with my training."

As Tim discovered upon arriving at the base of Mt. Rainier, he wasn't the only one who had worked hard to prepare for the climb. For instance, he was mightily impressed with the preparation of one of his climbing partners, Dr.

Maury Oswald, age fifty-four, and a family practice physician from Anchorage, Alaska.

Just a year earlier, Dr. Oswald couldn't even walk around the block in his neighborhood, let alone climb a mountain. Sickened by pancreatitis caused by his blood pressure medication, Dr. Oswald, at 280 pounds, was so weak and out of shape that treading just a few steps proved exhausting.

"I let myself go when I knew better," Dr. Oswald said. "Not only am I a physician, but I also have a BS in nutrition and I was a fair athlete as a young man, having played baseball at the semi-pro level. In short, I knew better. But life happens—marriage, children, career—and the next thing I knew, I was a fat nutritionist."

After Dr. Oswald struggled to simply walk around the zoo with his kids, he decided to turn his life around and began a quest to lose one pound every week. He also set an audacious goal for himself: to eventually summit Mt. Rainier.

Before every climb of this magnitude, climbers and their hired guides engage in an exhaustive gear check to guarantee their equipment will uphold the rigors of unpredictable conditions. "When I met Maury at the gear check for our Rainier climb," Tim raved, "he had lost fifty-four pounds in fifty-four weeks and was ready to summit the mountain. And he did! It was truly an awe-inspiring achievement."

"I had a significant adverse health event, and I turned my life around," Dr. Oswald said. "I am now off my blood pressure medicine, and my cholesterol levels are terrific. I believe what I have done in the last fourteen months is within the grasp of most people in declining health, due to issues of weight management. It boils down to simply eating less, eating right, and exercising more."

As Dr. Oswald and numerous other leaders in this chapter have demonstrated, setting a goal is imperative for your fitness success. He implores others to forge ahead with a fitness plan and audacious goals to aggressively move toward the fitness lives they imagine. "If I can do it, most anyone can!"

SUCCESS HABIT: Fitness

"About eighteen years ago, I started walking two miles a day, five mornings a week with my neighbor. We have come to appreciate all four seasons and enjoyed many beautiful sunrises on our early morning walks. You become pretty good friends with someone you have walked literally thousands of miles with over the years, so it is much more than a physical benefit, but mental as well. When people ask me about walking, the first thing I encourage them to do is to find a committed walking partner to help them stick with it and to make it fun."

SUCCESS HABIT: Fitness

"We take a Sunday family tour. A deeply rooted Norwegian success habit is to get everyone out of the house on Sunday—from toddlers to grandparents. Hike in the summer and cross country ski in the winter. Take brisk walks that are longer than the US version (the distance from the refrigerator to the TV)."

SUCCESS HABIT: Fitness

"For the past fourteen years, I've volunteered to coach Peewee hockey (ages eleven to twelve) because it's a great way for me to skate and get some exercise, too. I loved to play hockey when I was a kid, but I've also seen too many bad coaches wreck the fun of playing for some kids. I try to make sure kids on our teams have a fun and productive learning experience."

Seven Fs

Faith

Family

Finances

Fitness

Friends

Fun

Future

The traditional wedding vow, "for better or worse, in sickness and in health, 'til death do us part," seems to apply more to friendships these days than marriage. We all have heroic images of friendships that have lasted through cancer, job loss, sibling warfare, and divorce.

For many of us, that heroic image of friends has been shaped by television shows like *M*A*S*H*, *Golden Girls*, *Cheers*, and *Friends*. Sitcoms like these make us yearn for close friendships like those of Pierce and Honeycutt—or even Phoebe, Monica, and Rachel. Even when friends like these fight like siblings and tease each other mercilessly, it's with the expectation that they will be there for one another, no matter what.

Clearly, Americans love TV shows about friendships. So why, then, are real friendships in decline? Our Seven Fs survey respondents indicated:

- Their friendships were not as satisfying as other areas in their lives.

- Almost half (45 percent) reported moderate to low satisfaction with friends.

- Men were even less satisfied with friendships than women.

That mirrors a recent American Sociological Review (ASR) study on friendships highlighted in *USA Today*. According to the survey results, Americans have been suffering a steady decline in the quality and quantity of friendships since 1985.

Anecdotally, evidence suggests we are turning more toward our families for our safety net and sense of camaraderie. It's tough to tell whether that's good or not. Every parent wants their kids to have good friends. And each half of a healthy marriage wants the other half to have good friends.

But the ASR study ups the ante for society. Researchers discovered a direct link between the decline in the quality of friendships and an increase in psychological and physiological problems. The point? Without good friends, we are less healthy.

Why the decline in quality friendships? There are many sensible speculations. One is that we are living through an explosion of communication technology. Not long ago, people actually gathered together to listen to music. Now we put iPods in our ears. In the 1980s, video games resembled pinball machines and bar tables—people had to interact in public to play. Cable television entertainment was a faint concept. When ESPN came on the scene in 1979, there were roughly thirty channels on a basic cable package. Today, there are hundreds of channels offering a compelling smorgasbord of shows to watch—alone.

Suburban sprawl hasn't helped much either. Sidewalks are gone, because we can't walk to anywhere significant. We're cocooning in our minivans, twenty minutes from home, so the kids can get together for soccer practice over the dinner hour. The front porch has been replaced by the glamorous back deck—we are learning from lifestyle magazines how to landscape the backyard so we can sit by ourselves and enjoy the view. Without a front porch, people don't just drop by much anymore . . . probably because it's not in the schedule!

One woman who replied to the Seven Fs survey shared her strategy for battling the backyard deck hermit syndrome. She and her husband signal to the neighbors that they are ready to get together with their neighbors by placing a pink flamingo in their front yard a couple times every month. Reflecting the modern-day era, she also uses Facebook to virtually send a "pink flamingo is in the front yard tonight" message. Whoever shows up gets a beer—and a friendship booster shot.

But We're Always Connected

There is no denying that mobile phones and texting help us stay in touch with friends. In some ways, we are more efficient with our precious time than ever before. We get a kick out of texting photos and sending inside jokes and even love notes via mobile devices. Paul especially enjoyed crowing about his first hole-in-one in golf by texting pictures to people in his cell phone's contact list. He later said the notes he received from people he hadn't seen in years were almost as fun as the real deal.

However, people we interviewed for this book talked of how the benefits of our e-gadgets were often usurped by those little dingers in our pockets. It's so tempting to respond to the ping of an iPhone or Blackberry. We are tested all day long with emails, texts, Tweets, sports updates, stock market blips, or reminders for appointments. In moments of weakness, when we succumb to the need to know what's going on, the people in our presence suffer.

Shut Down, Power Off

What's happened to the value of good, old-fashioned, uninterrupted face-to-face connections? And how do people find balance between their meaningful relationships and friendships and the constant barrage of immediate e-communications? Dan Mallin has found a solution that works for him. He and his wife have created a technology-free zone for their family and friends in their North Woods cabin, which they affectionately call "Log-off."

Ironically, Mallin is the poster child for the uber-connected work style. He was first in line for an iPhone and again for the iPad. His voicemail says, "The best way to get a hold of me is to email me at. . . ." He and his business partner, Scott Litman, are reshaping the marketing and advertising services landscape through a virtual agency called Magnet 360. He and his other partner, his wife Deb, are taking care of reshaping their hectic lives.

When Mallin and his family and friends need to get away, they visit his northern Wisconsin lake home, where no one is allowed to plug in or log on. There is no TV. At the entrance to the property is a large pine log with the words "log off" carved into the side. "Even though I have grown up completely comfortable with 24/7 communication technology, I still appreciate the time with family and friends where we shut the gadgets off," he explained. "'Log-off' is an attitude as much as a place."

What Pulls You Together?

It's easier to maintain friendships by uniting in a common purpose, especially when that means you see your friends through scheduled activity. Many of our survey respondents admitted they are much more likely to be a good friend when they see their friends consistently at work, church, or service clubs. We know that when we have a regular cadence of getting together, we are much more responsible about cultivating and fertilizing the friendships we cherish. It's disconcerting to think of ourselves as out-of-sight-is-out-of-mind types of friends. But there's comfort in knowing others claim the same character flaw!

Tim said, "Paul and I met while serving on a nonprofit board of directors—an experience conducive to creating lasting friendships. We met four times each year, with a Thursday evening dinner, an overnight stay, and a six-hour meeting on Friday. Through our board work, we learned of our hopes, dreams, and values."

It was the board duties that helped conceive this book. We were asked to present an inspirational program for our nonprofit agency's two hundred plus managers. We chose to talk publicly for the first time about the Seven Fs. It was a transformational experience for both of us as speakers. Neither of us had ever experienced that level of intimacy and riveting attention from such a large audience. While walking a golf course hours later, Paul turned and said, "We should write a book on the Seven Fs." And so we have!

Working Harder Now Than Ever

Like many people nearing the empty-nest syndrome, we're working harder to stay connected to a small circle of close friends. Through our twenties and thirties, we were so wrapped up in growing careers, raising good kids, and nurturing great marriages that we let some friendships slide. There were plenty of wonderful people in our lives through work, kids' stuff, church, volunteering, golf, and beyond. But we could have done far better at being good friends.

Our own survey indicates differing degrees of satisfaction with friendship based on age. Those who are younger than twenty-five or older than sixty indicated strong satisfaction with their friendships, while those ages twenty-six to fifty-nine rated their satisfaction lower.

The friendship study mentioned earlier in this chapter claims most adults identify two hundred people they consider friends over the course of their lifetimes. About thirty of those people would be considered good friends, and about six would be considered best friends.

Bob Beaudine has developed an interesting way of thinking about close friends, whom he calls one's "inner circle." Beaudine is the author of a wonderful book called *The Power of WHO*, in which he provides insight on how our friendships evolve and grow.

Beaudine describes the inner circle as twelve floating friends—people you love from different places in your life who are unlikely to ever get together. These twelve "have a special place in your heart," but communication is sporadic. From that twelve, there are three friends with whom you have a deeper connection, your communication is more consistent, and you depend on each other for specific things in your life. And from that group is the one friend whom Beaudine describes as providing "a deep kinship that transcends even family at times."

> It's not surprising to learn that friends have a very large effect on how satisfying we find our jobs.

We have found it's helpful to simply diagram Beaudine's twelve/three/one friendship dynamic in our own lives and ask the question: "What can I do to help these special people?"

Because we spend so much of our time working, it's not surprising to learn that friends have a very large effect on how satisfying we find our jobs. Tom Rath is a researcher with the Gallup Organization who wrote a book called *Vital Friends: The People You Can't Afford to Live Without*. Gallup has interviewed more than 5 million people about their work lives.

In a *USA Today* interview, Rath made this important observation: "When we think about improving our lives, we focus our development inward. But the real energy occurs in each connection between two people, which can bring about exponential returns."

With a best friend at work, we are seven times more likely to be engaged with the company's mission, get more done in less time, have fewer mistakes and accidents, be more innovative, and build deeper relationships with customers. In short, employee satisfaction is nearly 50 percent higher when we have close friends at work.

The big news for business leaders is the effect to the bottom line. Rath continued, "When we asked people if they would rather have a best friend at work or have a 10 percent pay raise, having a friend clearly won." So, there is evidence that friends keep us healthy, personally and professionally.

Venus and Mars

Long before late-night talk comedians poked fun at the quirkiness of the opposite sexes, men and women have approached their friendships in strikingly different ways. Obviously we build male–female friendships through the normal course of living, but the way we like to hang out within the privacy of one's own gender can be downright hilarious (at least to members of the other gender)!

One married woman shared that her favorite way to hang out with girlfriends was to travel to her lake cabin. "When I get together with my girlfriends, I want to take my bra off and sit around for hours drinking wine and talking face-to-face with my girls," she explained. "If even one guy shows up, it ruins the whole thing." Another fifty-three-year-old female banker from Atlanta shared a similar perspective, "For me, a thirty-minute belly laugh with my girlfriends is better than sex."

Guys, on the other hand, prefer to sit side-by-side, focused more on play—watching a game, casting a fishing line, or sharing a golf cart. It's more about the shared experiences and less about the conversation.

In one of our favorite "bromance" references, five guys talk of a continuous Thursday night poker game where the only rule was no talking about work or family. In the tenth year, one guy asked another, "I'm just curious; do you even know the names of my kids?"

Without a pause, the guy quipped, "No, but I'll rename them if you don't shut up and deal!"

Friend "Blender"

It may seem difficult to think of interacting with our friends in a more business-like fashion—or even doing business with them. Paul Koch, the managing partner of one of the leading wealth advisory teams at UBS, has rejected the common wisdom that one shouldn't do business with friends.

"Twenty years ago, I made it one of my life goals to deliberately do business with my friends," Koch said. We've all been warned that we should never do business with our friends because what will happen if something goes wrong?

"I wanted to accept the challenge of making sure we do business in such a way that I'd never lose a friend," he continued. "I consider that to be the highest standard of service. Today, I have so much fun with my work. We counsel our friends about their finances—and we spend time dining together, traveling together, getting our families together, and discussing what dreams they have for their future. I take pride in blending as many Fs as I can at one time."

Thinking of You

One of the simplest friendship gestures is simply staying in touch—reaching out with an "I'm thinking of you" message of any kind. Facebook is quickly becoming the friendship connection of choice. People of all ages are converging through this one magical media.

> Facebook is quickly becoming the friendship connection of choice.

Paul's son threw a twentieth birthday party for himself by posting a notice on Facebook in the morning for a pizza party that night at a pizza joint ten miles away. Without talking to anyone, more than thirty people showed up—one even drove three hours to get there! Even Mom and his sisters knew about it. When Paul laughed and labeled the whole thing as a stunt, his son said, "How else would I have gotten the word out?"

We shouldn't be surprised. Every day, groups are forming on Facebook to help friends stay connected. College classmates prepare for class reunions by sharing pictures and memories. Church choirs share performance schedules and YouTube clips of potential new songs because choir members are more motivated when they weigh in on the choice of songs. And a personal favorite: the inventor of a contractor's tool, the Handy Paint Pail, has developed a Facebook page to help do-it-yourselfers share stories and ideas about how they use their favorite Handy Paint Pail products. Some of the frequent contributors have even become "friends"—go figure!

Joseph Martinez understood. He's a happy, successful property management professional in Orange County, California. He has kept many strong friendships by persistently staying in touch.

"I'm not much of a Facebook guy," Martinez said. "But I've found keeping up with my friends to be one of the most rewarding parts of my life." Part of Martinez's secret is approaching each friendship independently.

"I've learned I have to think about different people at different times in the day," he said. "Some friends are only available in the morning and others later in the day. Some we go back and forth by texting . . . others we talk by phone. I take a lot of pride in knowing what is going on in their lives."

Staying in touch increases Martinez's probability that surface-level check-ins will sprout into substantial connections. He explained, "Most of the time we are just casually catching up, talking about the same old stuff, but every once in awhile we have surprises to share. I love listening to people who are energized by the events of their lives. I feel like I share their success. And other times, we really need to pick each other up. Everyone struggles with job loss or relationships that are strained. You know? Business comes and goes. We change jobs, careers, even where we live. But we keep the same friends. Without good friendships, my life would be much less satisfying."

"Seeing" Friends

Sawubona is a Zulu way of saying, "hello" that literally means, "I see you." The producers of the movie *Avatar* leveraged that simple definition into a powerfully emotional message. At pivotal moments, the main characters look each other in the eyes and offer the words, "I see you," with the sincerity of a prayer.

As the story unfolds, we learn the luxurious triple meaning of *sawubona*. First, it means "I see into you—into your soul, to the very essence of you." Second, it means, "I see into you, and I respect you for who you are—not for what you do or what you are going to become, but for who you are right now." And third, it means, "I cherish your gifts and your presence."

When was the last time you expressed the "I see you" concept to anyone? I respect you for who you are right now, and I cherish your gifts and your presence. How much more healthy could your relationships be if your friends knew you cared for them in this way?

Really good friends are important because they can see things that a spouse or immediate family member is too close to see. As Tim explained, "I'm usually a very happy, optimistic guy. But there are times when I really need my friends to be my cheerleaders. Sometimes life is hard! When I am down on myself, waning in my faith, and listening too much to the negative self-talk, I have a small circle of good friends who can pull me up out of the gutter in ways that my wife can't. I understand the metaphor of the deep well of despair. When we sink down into that well, it's a very special thing when friends can pull us up and out of that well to see the sunlight."

Men or women, young or old, deep down inside we all know that one of the greatest benefits of a good friendship is feeling well listened to and encouraged. There is no magic wand for really good friendships—just one strong message: what really works is making the time to give the proper attention to being a good friend.

SUCCESS HABIT: Friends

"My wife and I have learned to embrace the French word *convive*. It means to thoroughly enjoy a fine meal with good friends. About twice a year, we sit down and discuss which friends we really want to 'convive' with. We deliberately invite interesting people who we believe will equally enjoy talking about our hopes and dreams, our children, and our values. We schedule months in advance. Sometimes we host in our home; sometimes we go out to a restaurant. Regardless, we always have great wine and we always turn the cell phones off."

SUCCESS HABIT: Friends

"Birthdays are a really big deal for me because I had a very small family and we didn't celebrate many birthdays. So I keep track of the birthdays of all my friends on my Google calendar. I set reminders ahead of time, and I make a point to send handwritten cards by mail and call my friends on their birthdays. When it's possible, we get together and laugh as much as we can. I'm old enough now that I am celebrating at least three birthdays a month, and that helps keep me connected with lots of friends."

SUCCESS HABIT: Friends

"Every second weekend in October is hunting weekend for my college buddies. We have a tired, old hunting shack that only a bunch of guys could appreciate. The five of us have a pact that keeps us coming back year after year. The only acceptable excuse for missing hunting weekend is a wedding or a funeral. It's been seventeen years in a row with none of us missing. One guy flies in from California every year. My wife has the same thing with her girlfriends the second weekend in November, except they go to a spa in Vegas."

Seven Fs

6

Faith

Family

Finances

Fitness

Friends

Fun

Future

Night after night, a busy executive came home to his family with two briefcases full of work. One night, as he began to prepare for another evening of paperwork, his son asked the mom, "Why does Daddy always have work to do when he gets home?"

The boy's mom replied, "Because Daddy can't get it all done at the office."

The young boy innocently quipped, "Why don't they put Daddy in the slower class?"

Guilty! We often find ourselves feeling compelled to keep the work mojo going late into the evening at the expense of experiencing the fun that life offers. We allow our workaholic tendencies and busyness to fill our lives and squeeze out the very reasons we work hard—fun with our families and our friends and recharging our own batteries. When we're having fun, we feel guilty about not working, and when we're working, we're thinking about not investing time with those we love.

In James Patterson's best-selling novel *Suzanne's Diary for Nicholas*, we learn the wonderful story of a busy mother and doctor named Suzanne who struggles with a terminal illness due to a heart condition. She makes dramatic changes to structure her life in ways that blend her work life with the joy of authentic relationships. As expected, Suzanne dies at a young age, and the following is discovered in her diary, intended for her young son, Nicholas:

> Imagine life is a game in which you are juggling five balls. The balls are called work, family, health, friends, and integrity. And you are keeping all of them in the air. But one day you finally come to understand that work is a rubber ball. If you drop it, it will bounce back. The other four balls—family, health, friends, and integrity— are made of glass. If you drop one of these, it will be irrevocably scuffed, nicked or perhaps even shattered. And once you truly understand the lesson of the five balls, you will have the beginnings of balance in your life.

So often we peer at life through a long plastic straw called *work* that we don't realize the fun opportunities we are missing or ignoring along the way. However, many people we interviewed for this book blew up the myopic straw and exposed all of the joys and fun that life has to offer.

They were living a blended life where fun and joy were the deliberate outcome of most of their life's journey—including work! They were pursuing the life they had imagined by consciously baking fun into the recipe of life. It was energizing to visit with them and to learn from their modeling.

In this chapter, we hope to inspire and encourage you to seek out and create more fun—however you define "fun."

What Is Fun?

When was the last time you laughed so hard that tears ran down your cheeks, your stomach ached, and every life stressor was suddenly stripped from your mind?

Perhaps instead you've enjoyed the sublime experience of curling up in your favorite chair on a cool winter evening with a stimulating book, a glass of wine, and zero distractions.

Or maybe you've experienced the joy of working alongside friends or family serving meals for the poor or packing nutritional meals to send to third world nations.

Are any of these your idea of fun?

Maybe yes, but maybe no. Unlike the other Seven Fs, which rely in part on societal norms, fun is entirely self-defined. Your idea of fun may be completely different from ours, and vice versa.

Fun is the all-important extra that catapults the other Fs from ordinary to extraordinary. When our faith, family, finances, friends, and future are injected with fun, life becomes a holistic blast! And when fitness, for example, is paired with fun, our interest in fitness increases and our health improves, and we'll likely live longer.

Fun and Health

Humor, laughter, and fun are effective holistic medications to stave off illness, relieve stress, boost our immune systems, and maintain a young perspective. A recent report found that people with heart disease were 40 percent less likely to laugh compared with people of the same age without heart disease. It's no wonder that "Laughter, the Best Medicine" has long been one of the most popular sections of the magazine *Reader's Digest*. For more than 7 million subscribers, it really is medicine.

> A recent report found that people with heart disease were 40 percent less likely to laugh . . .

Busyness was a strong theme as a barrier to fun. Work and family responsibilities can consume our every waking minute if we let them. As a result, we need to zealously carve out opportunities for fun. One male executive coach shared with us: "For nearly two decades I only focused on my family and career—fun with my buddies just wasn't part of the equation. I stopped hunting, playing basketball, going to rock concerts—everything! Thankfully, they kept calling me back and today we're a major source of fun for each other again."

Fun permeates the atmosphere of the Mocha Monkey coffee shop in the lakeside community of Waconia, Minnesota. It has a vibe that Starbucks and other McCoffee shops would love to clone. The charming atmosphere that's been created in this historic one-hundred-year-old home draws people to let their hair down with their friends. Many customers find it fun to get lost in the nooks and crannies with a good book. Some find fun in attending a poetry reading or acoustic concert. "We know people are having fun, because unlike other coffee shops, we are constantly hearing hearty laughter, and that makes this place special," said Jon Schmidt, the shop's owner.

When it comes to the positive effect of fun on our health, no fun is simply not an option. Consider the advice of Dr. Sidney Freedman, the fictional psychiatrist who regularly visited the *M*A*S*H* 4077th: "Ladies and gentlemen, take my advice: pull down your pants and slide on the ice."

Humor as a Coping Mechanism

There wasn't any ice below ground in Copiapo, Chile, for thirty-three miners to slide on. But as it turned out, the Sidney Freedman style sense of humor was one of two key ingredients to survival for the triumphant miners. Entombed 2,000 feet underground for sixty-nine days in October 2010, they survived the longest underground entrapment in human history.

Following their historic rescue, each told tales of faith and laughter as their key to hope and sanity. Together, they found ways to joke around and preserve a little bit of fun in the darkness.

Hopefully, none of us will be faced with those horrendous circumstances in our lifetimes. However, we have all felt emotions of isolation, emptiness, and hopelessness. Fun helps fight back against the negative power of those emotions. It worked for the miners, and it can work for all of us.

One Person's Pleasure Is Another's Pain

Professional golfers live a life that is stark contrast to Chilean miners. However, golf is one of those activities that causes many people to vacillate wildly on the pleasure and pain scale. For weekend hackers, we don't really find too much pain. But what about when golf is your job?

Kris Tschetter is a professional golfer who successfully maintained her LPGA tour status for nearly twenty-five years. "There were plenty of better players than me when I was in college who should have been better pros than me," she explained. "But somehow, I was able to stay focused on the fun in being a professional golfer . . . getting past the parts of the lifestyle and the performance pressure that others just couldn't handle."

Yes, when Kris goes to work, she's playing golf, and golf is fun! However, the professional golf pressure and demanding travel routine can drive out most of the fun, especially when you're not playing well. Most professional golfers are away from home and family at least thirty weeks a year. And there are no salaries in golf. Half of the players who start a tournament go home without a paycheck because they didn't play well enough to make the cut. With the pressure and lots of idle time, many younger players struggle to find the fun, and they can't make a living.

"My first year on tour, I remember hearing another player telling someone that playing golf for a living wasn't fun. She said it was her job! I decided right then and there that I would quit the tour if I couldn't think of it as more fun than work." Kris told us she always traveled with a good book to combat the airline hassles. And she had deliberately invested time to make friends in each of the LPGA tour cities. "The fun for me is to embrace each of the sites. The international travel is really tough, but I love to visit foreign grocery stores and bring home treats that people can't find anywhere else in the world. Then, when I'm playing well, it gets even more fun."

Fun Family Traditions

Kirk Gassen is in his fourth year as CEO of Gassen Companies, one of the largest association management firms in the Midwest. Kirk and his wife, Jayne, have managed to inject plenty of rip-roaring family fun along with an ongoing rhythm of positive bonding traditions. Their kids, ages twenty, eighteen, fourteen, and ten, have grown accustomed to some of the familial antics that keep the fun meter on high and their household a "gass."

Nearly every night, the Gassens try to have dinner together as a family. "Even if it's 8 p.m., when the kids roll in from sports, dinner is a big deal around here," Kirk said. "And while at dinner, they play the 'best thing, worst thing' game to encourage everyone to share the highlights and lowlights from their day. And now, when friends join them for dinner, the friends invariably ask, 'Hey, can we play that silly best-thing game?'"

The Gassens also schedule an annual road trip to a Colorado dude ranch years in advance, and those dates are carved in stone. It's a special week every year with no distractions. "No TV, no cell service, and no Internet forces significant quality time to just . . . have . . . fun!" Kirk smiled.

Other great ideas from the Gassens:

- **Meals:** Sunday mornings in their household include a gigantic breakfast. Dad's in charge, and it's all made-to-order.

- **Birthdays:** Homemade cards are required, so that the family is personally communicating their support to one another.

- **Giving:** They all walk/run the Turkey Run on Thanksgiving Day to benefit others.

When the Kids are Away, the Parents Play!

Other families are dialing up the fun by creating traditions after the kids are out the nest. Empty nesters Jodi Harpstead and her husband, Stan, have created a lively tradition of dining with a small group of close friends over good food and great wine. "We have so many friends from our church, to the parents of our kids' friends, to our colleagues in our current jobs," she explained. "It's very rewarding to get people together at a different restaurant each month or so just to have fun. We love who we are when we are entertaining. And learning how to pair food and wine has been a blast!"

Recently, the Harpsteads began taking their dinner friends fly fishing. They went in on a deal with another couple to purchase a plot of land that surrounds a fly fishing stream. "Our group trips to our private fly fishing spot are fun for everyone," Stan said. "Some of us actually fish, some play catch with their dogs, and some read the newspaper. We all enjoy nature in a gorgeous setting." The Harpsteads are becoming excellent Seven Fs blenders.

Researching Fun

According to our survey research, while fun strongly correlated with "leading the life we imagine," it also ranked dead last among our top priorities. How could this be?

"This low-ranking fun score could be interpreted as people thinking they need to defer fun for later, and not now," said Dr. Gene Roeder, a clinical and forensic psychologist from Sacramento, California. "When does later become now? Fun can start now!"

Dr. Roeder credited a guest speaker during his graduate school education with helping him learn the discipline of scheduling time off. The president of the American Psychological Association was the speaker who urged the soon-to-be doctors to:

- Schedule your free time in advance or you'll risk being unhealthy and having workaholic tendencies.

- Take time for decompression and regeneration.

- Find a passion that creates fun.

The speaker's idea of fun was scuba diving, because no one could talk to him underwater!

Roeder's adult daughter finally convinced him to put his fun money where his mouth was by embarking on a sixteen-mile kayaking adventure off the coast of Kauai in Hawaii.

In the six weeks following his commitment to his daughter and while preparing for the trip, Roeder lost twenty-three pounds. Having the goal made his workouts fun. "I love to have fun," Roeder said. "It's my basic approach to life. It takes discipline for me to NOT have fun, and now I need to work on the other Fs." As he spoke with us, he was heading out the door to an Eagles concert, scheduled far in advance.

Extreme Fun

Nancy Dahl is a forty-something corporate executive who is raising two adventurous boys. "We've learned to embrace our wild sides as a way to really have fun with our boys," she explained. As the president and chief operating officer of the world's largest professional school photography company, her day job is rather cerebral and sophisticated. Her weekends resemble the Speed Channel, because she likes to use small-engine horsepower to leave the stress of her job in the dust! She loves riding Harley Davidson motorcycles on the open road, racing ATVs and dirt bikes on the family farm, jumping watercrafts on the water at the lake cabin, and riding snowmobiles to the limit up and down mountain slopes.

Outdoor motor sports help blend her craving for adventure that most people don't have. "The combination of quality family time and our 'need for speed' blends two passions—family and fun. We especially like our adventure vacations. It's a great way to keep the family together and work off some steam. And I think it's really a hoot!" she laughed.

The Perfect Vacation

For many of us, fun is synonymous with taking vacations. And with limited time to escape from our daily routines, we want to make the most of our precious time off. Behavioral science is increasingly yielding insights into what we can do to make the most of our leisure time.

Drake Bennett of the *Boston Globe* supports this leisure research with a litany of counterintuitive examples. "For example, how long we take off probably counts for less than we think, and taking more short trips leaves us happier than taking a few long ones," Bennett said. "We're often happier planning a trip than actually taking it."

Other Bennett insights:

- **Finish:** How a trip ends matters more than how it begins.

- **Friends/Family:** Who you're with matters as much as where you go.

- **Memories:** If you want to remember a vacation vividly, do something during it that you've never done before.

With all the money we spend on vacations over our lifetimes, having a fun formula for vacations should increase the return on investment.

Philanthropic Fun

Mike Stensland, a top-tier financial advisor, has learned to masterfully blend finances and fun through philanthropy. Every Thanksgiving dinner, he and his wife, Molly, give each of their two children a sum of money with the understanding that it should be used to benefit others. At Christmas, they reveal to each other how they shared their money.

Their goal was to teach their young children the joy inherent in the value of generosity. Their role was to identify a family in need and donate their money in some form. They live by the motto: "To whom much is given, much is expected."

Stensland's favorite story is when his daughter learned of a family who had no money for Christmas presents. She used her money to hire a Santa Claus and deliver gifts.

Fun at Work

Lately, fun at work seems to be a declining value in many organizations.

With a dragging economy and a constant pressure for increased productivity, as dedicated employees, we often put our noses to the grindstone and ignore the return on investment that comes from investing in corporate culture and fun.

Research confirms this virtuous circle. Accomplishment creates joy, joy creates laughter, and laughter increases productivity. In a nutshell, good work creates joy and joy creates good work.

What is our role as leaders to drive a productive and engaging work environment? Employee loyalty and engagement are dramatically affected by whether people find purpose and enjoyment in their work. In many cases, they are spending more time at work than they are with their families. It's imperative to interject some fun into the workplace.

At a gathering of two hundred corporate and private business executives and workforce managers, Paul asked attendees which of the Seven Fs would most likely increase work satisfaction. Forty percent said "Fun," with "Future" a distant second. Even the leaders of our organizations yearn for more fun at work.

> *"I'm not proud of the fact that the pressure of my job was driving out my sense of fun at work."*

One leader finally relented to a suggestion of a bowling competition with his sales department. "I'm not proud of the fact that the pressure of my job was driving out my sense of fun at work," he said, "but I am glad that I woke up to see the light. I even paid for everyone's first game!"

We can all agree the economy has been challenging for business the last several years and brutal on charitable nonprofits, potentially making workdays less fun. "Yes, we have been facing a lot of pressure around here," explained Noel Raymond, co-director of the cultural community hub Pillsbury Neighborhood Services and Theatre. "We've been really squeezed because the people we serve are really hurting and their needs are increasing. We are being spread thinner and thinner. It's a classic formula for demoralization."

However, Raymond is an exceptional leader who won't let her followers slide into daily despair. "I've always believed that we have the ability to control whether or not we are enjoying our work," she explained. One of her most effective strategies is to get program participants working together on activities to take control of their difficult situations. Even under duress, people can find fun working together, sharing positive energy.

One of Raymond's national award-winning programs—the Chicago Avenue Project—engages children from rough neighborhoods in creating their own theater productions. "When we get our staff together to help produce a new show with the kids, we see that our work brings out the best in people," she said with pride. "That's fun, and it keeps us going."

The successes we've covered in this chapter were not the result of happenstance. They were the direct result of people deliberately injecting fun into their lives. The traditions of the Gassen family, the intentionality of the Harpsteads, the persistence of professional golfer Kris Tschetter, the planning of the Roeders, the adventure of the Dahls, and the philanthropy of the Stenslands were:

- Lined up with their values

- Successful in bringing friends or families together

- Planned far in advance

- Positive in moving toward the lives they imagined

To inject more fun into our lives, we must be more intentional. If we're not careful, busyness will take over and the fun and joy that we deserve will vanish into our monotonous routines.

What planning and scheduling do you need to add more fun in your life?

SUCCESS HABIT: Fun

"I'm a surgeon, and I've learned that I can't really relax and have fun unless I actually get away. I mean, really away. My favorite place is the mountains. It's very difficult not to have fun when you hike above 7,000 feet in the Wallowa Forest in Oregon. You can really relax and find the joy with mother nature. There have been times when I felt compelled to carry a solar panel on my backpack to power my laptop and Blackberry, but that would defeat the purpose!"

SUCCESS HABIT: Fun

"Each New Year's Day, I decide what new skill, sport, or class I would like to try. This new thing will become my carrot for completing tedious tasks I need to do. For example, this year I wanted to learn how to knit. I found a shop that has Saturday afternoon classes. Knowing that the class is waiting for me at the end of a work week helps me get through the hectic work week."

SUCCESS HABIT: Fun

"Make sure to have space in the schedule for doing 'nothing.' This sounds unproductive, but it fosters the self-care needed to be vibrant and creative: crucial elements for thriving! Doing nothing may be taking a walk just to take in some beauty, going to the library to look through magazines with no particular purpose in mind but to have fun, or sitting in silence to let your spirit rest in the life bigger than you. Remember that exercise, adequate sleep, and healthy eating are necessary for a balanced life."

Seven Fs

Faith

Family

Finances

Fitness

Friends

Fun

Future

Whitney Houston rocked the pop music charts in 1986 when she sang, "I believe that children are our future. Teach them well and let them lead the way."

A woman battling breast cancer wrote those powerful lyrics. Our society rallies around the "children are our future" theme because we yearn for peace to win out over violence, happiness over despair, and health over famine. That's why so many of us give our time and money to education, medical research, and compelling social causes.

Hope is the central concept of future—the optimistic belief that we are building a better, safer tomorrow for ourselves and others. Hope explains the existence of more than 70 million baby boomers who were born to World War II parents. Hope propelled astronauts to the moon. And it likely drives much of your day-to-day decision-making.

Satisfaction with future ranked second, behind family, on our Seven Fs survey. Survey participants under age thirty had the highest degree of satisfaction with their future. While not surprising, it's still a positive sign for all of us.

Perhaps the most interesting survey reply to future was how people answered the question: "Which F best describes how you think about your work?" Future was the second-highest motivator, eclipsed only by finances. Despite a constant stream of negative news reports, it seems as if we are embracing our collective responsibility to leave the world in better shape than when we arrived.

Throughout the course of our interviews, three major themes surfaced regarding the future:

1. Ensuring the rights of all children to a quality education

2. Building healthy local and global communities

3. Finding one's personal purpose in helping others

Curiosity as a Gateway

Ian Walmsley, PhD, is one of the leaders guiding the future of Oxford University in Oxford, England. As professor of experimental physics and head of Oxford's department of atomic and laser physics, Walmsley "works on stuff that we can't even dream about using commercially for at least thirty to fifty years," said one Oxford student.

Although Walmsley is distinctly British, he gained an appreciation for Americans' "can-do" future-oriented perspective while working as director of the Institute of Optics in Rochester, New York. "In America, I observed the general attitude of people to be very optimistic, in the sense that they believe they can achieve anything they set their minds to," he said. "That's very positive, and yet it also creates a self-inflicted pressure where students can get in their own way." He finds Oxford to be an artful mix of American spirit and other cultural influences where people are less intense, worried, or fretful.

"Genuine curiosity is central to how ideas become the progress for our future," Walmsley explained. He described a profound sense of responsibility for creating the right climate for students to thrive at Oxford.

"Some families send their children halfway around the globe to Oxford to be with us for years on end. We need to ensure people can exchange ideas, argue, and debate freely and safely," Walmsley shared. "Education is not a theory, it's about practical day-to-day demonstrations of healthy curiosity."

Does Higher Education Still Pay?

As Walmsley acknowledged, paying for college is a significant stretch for most families. And yet, higher education is still one of the best investments you can make in your future. The earnings potential of an average college graduate is calculated to be four to twenty times above an average high school graduate's earnings, depending on the survey source.

The bottom line: a high school education gives job applicants a decided advantage over those who don't finish high school. And a college degree multiplies that advantage

> *"As a young, single woman, I deliberately invested in my own education."*

significantly. Even if we discount the obvious salary advantage, the best companies will always want the most qualified workers, and those companies will be the most likely to provide valuable health care benefits and employer-sponsored retirement plans.

"As a young, single woman, I deliberately invested in my own education," explained one Seven Fs focus group participant. "After college, I got my PhD to make sure I would have basic security . . . that I wouldn't be overly dependent upon any one person, except myself. Now I have a wonderful family and a great job in consulting. The investment was totally worth it in so many ways."

We Have No Choice

Yet we also know that for some kids, a future filled with good job opportunities, let alone college, can often be a distant dream. That's what Adrienne Diercks, founder and executive director of Project Success, meant when she said, "I am challenged the most by future."

Diercks is a highly regarded leader who helps develop the aspirations of urban kids in middle school and high school. Eighteen years into Project Success, she and her team touch more than 10,000 urban school kids every year—and another 40,000 if you count their families. The program uses live theater to demonstrate and help kids dream about what's possible in their lives.

"I believe that it's our job to make sure our kids see a healthy vision for their future. We have no choice but to work toward the idea that our children and families will have even better opportunities than we had as kids," Diercks shared.

Facilitated discussions after each theater production help kids and their families see unlimited possibilities for their lives. "The kids love the idea that they can change the pattern of their lives, and many embrace the idea that their education can help them create their own path," she said. "Every year, we keep getting more and more public and private support, which demonstrates how much people care about kids."

Teaching Responsibility

On another scale, curiosity and responsibility are alive and well in Oak Grove Middle School and pouring out onto the streets of Bloomington, Minnesota and communities around the nation.

That's because Oak Grove schoolteachers Renee Corneille and Kathleen West resolved to transform the tragedy of 9/11 into an unforgettable learning experience for their students. West's uncle was Thomas Burnett Jr.—one of the heroes of hijacked United Airlines Flight 93 who kept their plane from becoming a weapon of mass destruction. Burnett grew up in Bloomington and attended its public schools.

"Less than a year after Tom's death, Kathleen and I decided that as teachers we had to do something to help the kids understand what it meant to die for your country," Corneille explained. "Tom died defending the civil liberties of a free society. Our responsibility to Tom's sacrifice is to learn how to be responsible citizens."

Because of Corneille and West's leadership, many school districts around the United States now rally their eighth-grade students around the Thomas Burnett Jr. Day of Service. One day a year, all of the eighth graders in participating schools pour out into the community and volunteer. And throughout the year, they complete specific course work designed to increase civic responsibility.

Recently, a graduate school researcher confirmed the positive effect of the Thomas Burnett Jr. Day of Service curriculum on kids. High school seniors who participated in the Day of Service curriculum as eighth graders were significantly more likely to be curious about their world and to volunteer in ways to help make their community better.

Dramatic end-of-life stories can be powerful motivators.

"I think Thomas Burnett Jr.'s family can be proud that his impact on the future didn't end with his life," Corneille said. "I can say with the highest confidence, this is the most important thing I will do in my career as a teacher."

Dramatic end-of-life stories can be powerful motivators that propel people into future-oriented endeavors. Danny Thompson was a charismatic Major League Baseball shortstop in the 1970s for the Minnesota Twins and Texas Rangers. Thompson continued to play at a very high level—even while he was fighting to stay alive.

Thompson was diagnosed with leukemia in 1974, but continued to play baseball for the next three seasons, including leading American League shortstops in hitting in 1975. Thompson played until the end of the 1976 season and died less than ten weeks later at age twenty-nine.

In 1977, Baseball Hall of Fame player Harmon Killebrew, a former teammate of Thompson's, and Ralph Harding, a former Idaho congressman, launched the Danny Thompson Memorial Golf Tournament in Idaho to benefit leukemia and cancer research. Today, the tournament has raised more than $10 million directly and another $25 million in matching grants, having a significant effect on cancer research.

"When Danny died, leukemia was virtually incurable," explained Georgie Fenton, tournament director. "Today, the recovery rate is almost 70 percent, with even greater hopes for the future."

Nicholas Lives On

Nicholas lived only a few hours. He and his twin brother, were born full-term, strong and healthy. However, Nicholas ran short of oxygen during delivery, and died later in the care of a top-notch regional hospital. After careful investigation, hospital executives acknowledged Nicholas's death was preventable and a direct result of errors made during the delivery process.

"The physician in charge and the hospital's CEO were sincerely remorseful and humbly apologetic," his mother recalled. "It was clearly a case of medical malpractice that yielded the offer of a financial settlement of life-changing money."

"It didn't take long for my husband and me to realize that no amount of money was going to bring Nicholas back to us," she continued. "Living under the weight of so much money, and knowing we had received it because Nicholas died, was not how we wanted to honor our son's short life."

Instead, the couple turned down the prospect of a huge settlement and became catalysts for changes at the hospital to help ensure a similar tragedy would not befall another family. Nicholas's mother applied her professional training in leadership and organizational development to partner with the CEO and his staff to create a central monitoring system for the Operating Room, and renovate several of the hospitals processes—specifically related to personal patient care for high risk patients. All these changes were driven from a simple vision, and a values platform of humility.

Since the tragic miscue, the hospital's CEO continues to provide regular updates to the family. His first letter included this message:

> *I can tell you in no uncertain terms that we will do everything in our power to carry your message forward and will consider your son's legacy in everything we do. It is little to ask given the incredible loss your family has suffered. And as you requested, we will update you with progress reports and the status of our improvements on a regular basis. We owe it to you, and to our broader community, to be there for the many families who trust us with the care of their loved ones.*

The couple still experiences a range of emotions, but also learned that while the ways of expressing discontent are limited, the ways to make a positive difference are boundless. "At times, we still feel profound frustration, deep sadness, and anger, but we also have a sense of peace and the ability to look forward in hope," his mother said. "Today, Nicholas's life is a light in our lives, and a way to send positive energy into the world."

Someday, Nicholas's twin brother will understand the heroic efforts of his parents. And hopefully, he will feel the effect his fallen brother made on future generations.

Seeing Potential

Tim watched his parents model a humble and honorable life to help ensure the future for others—half a world away from their origins and relatives. "We moved as a family to Asia when I was a small child," he explained.

Tim's parents were missionaries who were originally going to work at an international school. But his dad left the school to help secure the future of Vietnamese refugees in Hong Kong.

"I saw my dad work with these amazing kids who were literally orphaned at the hands of their own parents," Tim continued. The children were placed in dilapidated boats on the shores of Viet Nam, with at least forty other people in each boat. They would drift on the sea in hopes of landing a better life in Hong Kong. Some survived the trip; others did not.

"It was a huge sacrifice and a remarkable ministry. It taught me that my faith and my commitment to a hopeful future is as much about the dirty work of my hands and feet as it is about my prayers and philanthropy," Tim said.

Mark Peterson recalled a similarly pointed moment with his father that provided direction and encouragement for his own life.

"My father was near death in a hospital bed," said Peterson, a retired nonprofit executive. "The last time I visited him, he introduced me to his nurse. He said, 'This is my son. I don't know what he's going to do with his life. But I know he's going to make life better for all of us—wherever we are.'"

That encouragement propelled Peterson to serve as CEO of one of the most progressive and effective social service entities in the United States, touching the lives of more than 100,000 people every year.

Encouraging Youth

College kids today are described as millennials by sociologists. The media has coined that same group, ages eighteen to twenty-nine, as the "We Generation" because they are the most socially altruistic of any generation on record.

To illustrate the millennials' perspective, they love their Starbucks, but hate the use of paper cups because they end up in landfills. Millennials are aggressive consumers, but they scan websites to check out the moral character and environmental effect of corporations before they spend their money with a particular company or organization.

The Pew Research Center has confirmed the millennials' entry into the workforce is the most challenging for any young adult generation since the Depression. And yet, this group is still optimistic about the future—and ours. In true character, this is the first generation reacting to the rejection of job interviews by embracing social entrepreneurism as a life mission that creates a steady, albeit sometimes smaller, paycheck.

What is Social Entrepreneurship?

Babson College in Massachusetts is developing a reputation for helping kids in their twenties build careers to solve people and planet problems while generating societal and economic value.

One of the best examples of what millennials are trying to encourage is TOMS Shoes. A young social entrepreneur named Blake Mycoskie founded the company in 2006. With each pair of TOMS Shoes sold, the company donates a new pair of shoes to a child in need.

Mycoskie got the idea from his adventures working as a cast member on the reality TV show *The Amazing Race*. While on location in Argentina, he fell in love with the Alpargata shoes made and worn by Argentinean farmers. He also noticed thousands of poor children working and playing without shoes.

Today, the company organizes shoe drops in some of the poorest places on the planet. As of September 2010, TOMS Shoes has given more than 1 million pairs of new shoes to children in twenty-five countries. The company is growing and is profitable.

Service Above Self

More than one hundred years ago, Rotary International was founded in Chicago based on the motto: "Service Above

Self." Today, Rotary is the oldest, largest, and most effective service club in the world. It has more than thirty-three thousand clubs worldwide, with Rotarians meeting once a week across the globe.

"Rotary changes lives," explained Mary Beth Growney Selene, who served as president of the Madison West Towne-Middleton Rotary club in Wisconsin. "It changes the lives of our members as much as the people we help."

The greatest example of Rotary's global effect is PolioPlus—the organization's flagship program to eradicate polio worldwide. Rotarians are partnering with UNICEF, the US Centers for Disease Control and Prevention, and the World Health Organization to eliminate the deadly disease from the planet. "Rotarians have contributed more than $900 million and countless volunteer hours to help immunize more than 2 billion children against the crippling and often fatal disease," Growney Selene said.

> "The eradication of the polio virus will be Rotary's lasting legacy to the children of the world."

Recently, the Bill and Melinda Gates Foundation offered a $355 million challenge grant to Rotary International to eliminate polio once and for all. By partnering locally and across the globe, Rotarians are peering into an unprecedented window of opportunity to make the world safer for all. "The eradication of the polio virus will be Rotary's lasting legacy to the children of the world," Growney Selene said. "And that's a future we can all be proud of."

Serving Oneself

Chris Nelson is a senior executive pastor who admits his vision of future is both selfish and selfless. His motivation is fundamentally about his need to make the most out of life.

"For me, future is about having a compelling reason to live fully, and die with nothing left in the tank," he explained. Today, Nelson is fifty-seven years old and said he still feels as young at heart as if he were as a teenager. He realized years ago that his self-perceived age was a factor of his attitude. And thus, he decided to do something about it by embracing the future as a diminishing resource.

"I've learned to embrace the future as something really, really important because how I want to live out my life and the impact I make for others will really define who I am today," Nelson said.

As a baby boomer, he's accustomed to how his generation has shaped society. For his own future sake, and for the benefit of those who are currently older than he is, he's focusing on enhancing living conditions for the elderly.

"I hope to influence people to understand that we can't warehouse our elders anymore. No one actually wants to be in a nursing home," Nelson said. "People my age have been changing society at every stage of our lives—most, but not all, of it good. At the very least, we want to age on our own terms, and we are working to reinvent society's norms."

He encouraged us all to think hard about our own commitments to future: "It's never too early or too late to dream about the future with high expectations. We only go around once. No one is too old to give. No one is too old to hug. No one is too old to reach out and help a friend. And you are never too old to try to change your world," Chris shared.

Looking Ahead

We never know when we'll have an effect on our kids, or vice versa. Paul recalled one of his favorite speaking engagements. "I was asked to speak to an integrated class of second, third, and fourth graders on the subject of writing a book on leadership," he explained. "I started by asking the question, 'What do good leaders do?'"

With striking clarity, a third-grade girl chirped, "They find a way to make things better for more people."

Her answer was one of those moments when Paul clearly received more than he gave as a volunteer. "In my work as an executive coach, her simple words of wisdom bounce through my mind frequently," he said. "The good leaders I know in my life are continually investing their hearts in the future. They persistently find ways to help make things better for more people."

At forty-seven years of age each (at the time of this writing), Tim and Paul are both basically at halftime in their lives—although not quite, if they live as long as Paul's grandmother (age 103!) or the centenarians studied in the Blue Zones.

We think people's satisfaction with their future, as expressed in the Seven Fs survey, is good news. Selfishly, we believe we need help in living a second half of our lives in a world that includes less scandal and greed, less terror and pollution, and more opportunity for people to live healthy lives and follow their dreams without fear.

What does a hopeful future look like for you?

SUCCESS HABIT: Future

"My husband and I have learned to schedule an annual meeting for ourselves every year, and we try to go to someplace exotic and warm. We think about our future by taking stock of our past year. We formally review what was fulfilling and what was a drain on us, and we create a new vision for the coming year. We have some really deep conversations. It helps us to think of happiness as a goal that we pursue together."

SUCCESS HABIT: Future

"My children are now grown and gone from our home. However, I still really love mothering. So one night a week, I have dinner at a nonprofit called Teen Challenge, which helps those who are battling substance abuse. I sit with troubled teenage girls for dinner. We talk, and I listen a lot. And I hold their hands and let them know that their lives won't always be this difficult. Dinner once a week is the least I can do, and I feel like I am really making a difference."

SUCCESS HABIT: Future

"At least one day a week, my father would lay out the newspaper on the kitchen table and wrestle us into having a discussion about what's going on in the world. That family activity taught me how to read a newspaper and helped me see that the world was much, much bigger than me. Today, I do something very similar with my kids . . . except we email and Twitter news items back and forth."

Summary

It's now up to you.

In the presence of new information, we often choose to change our behavior. That's the mission of this book. We hope you have learned something that's prompted you to take action toward the life you imagine.

Profound Is Often Simple

"So what's the main thing you learned through writing this book?" a friend asked us, while walking down the fourth fairway.

Our reply: "You have to schedule your priorities."

"That's it?" he blurted, as if expecting something more profound. It instantly created an awkward mood within our golfing foursome.

Two hours later, our questioning friend apologized. "I'm sorry to have jumped on your "schedule your priorities" insight earlier," he said. "Now that I think about it, there are things in my life that are really important, that I just don't get around to doing. As I reflect on my calendar now, what gets scheduled, gets done. I need to sit down with my wife and wrestle control of our schedule again. That's what I'm going to do tonight."

Tim said, "It reminds me of a quote I read by Archibald Hart: 'Humans were designed for camel travel, but most people are now acting like supersonic jets.'" In a nutshell, most of us are living at too fast a pace. The pace of modern life is stretching all of us beyond our limits. We are paying for this lifestyle in the hard and painful currency of stress and anxiety—plain and simple.

> *In this hurry up and go-get-'em society, we need to take personal accountability for how we spend our time.*

The simplest lesson: in this hurry up and go-get-'em society, we need to take personal accountability for how we spend our time and with whom we decide to share it. We're all overscheduled. It's a sign of the times.

There is no doubt we are happier if we block out more time for fun. We increase our calm if we sit down to discuss finances in the context of our dreams. We feel better if we protect our time for exercise every day. We are better friends if we guard our dinner dates like a momma bear protects her cubs.

Matt and Kari Norman understand ferocious schedule-protecting. Both are achievement-oriented thirty-something parents. Matt is president of one of the most successful Dale Carnegie Training franchises in North America. Kari is a dynamic work-at-home, power volunteer mom. As the couple was working through the dynamics of raising twin boys, they were constantly butting heads about important family matters. "Even though we talked about things at the dinner table every night, we were still getting our wires crossed," Matt explained.

"We are much better now, since discovering 'Family Business Night,' as we call it," Kari said. A mutual friend encouraged the young couple to set aside one hour each week to coordinate the family business and they've now established a very healthy ritual.

Once a week the Normans sit down with a glass of wine and discuss the family schedule three weeks in advance. They coordinate driving responsibilities and review social commitments. "One night, both Kari and I had four separate dinner date requests!" Matt shared. "It's not that we're super-popular. We just had lots of requests come in at once. Without "Family Business Night," we each would have made promises we couldn't keep, and that's what used to get us into trouble."

As the cover of our book indicates, we believe success with the Seven Fs comes when you blend the Seven Fs together naturally. The Norman's Family Business Night is an excellent example of how planning ahead helps make life's normal stresses blend together.

Blending

"The most articulate blending example for me is my involvement in Rotary," Paul explained. "With eighteen years as a Rotarian, I've learned so much about the kind of person I want to be when I grow up!"

The one hundred members in Paul's City of Lakes Rotary Club became a steady source of friends, clients, fun, faith sharing and community building. "What I have found in Rotary is a network of fun, humble people who exist to help each other," Paul said. "Rotary has been my most consistent commitment throughout my professional life, because it satisfies so many of my needs," he explained.

Through Rotary, the Batz family has hosted international exchange students, volunteered together and contributed to international relief efforts, including Haiti earthquake victims. "Without Rotary expanding my worldview, I'd still be that simple South Dakota boy who came with wide eyes to the big city!" Paul said.

In 2010, Paul was his Rotary club's first-ever delegate for a sister-city relationship with the Uppsala Östra Rotary Club in Sweden. "It's so cool, because our daughter Katie was studying at the University of Uppsala!" he said. "Now that's blending!"

Togetherness

If blending is helpful, so is the concept of togetherness. Nothing significant is ever accomplished alone.

Tim is a big fan of *The Power of WHO*, previously mentioned in Chapter 5. Reading author Bob Beaudine's philosophy about achieving personal and business success inspired Tim to leverage his relationships in more meaningful ways.

"I'm in a study group within our industry," Tim said. "After reading *The Power of WHO*, we each invested the time to build our bucket list—the one hundred things we want to do in our lives before we die." Tim was surprised to learn one of his colleagues, Chris, had the same wish on his bucket list: to climb Mt. Rainier. Within one year, Tim and his twenty-one-year-old son, Jon, joined Chris in Washington State and they checked that item off their bucket lists.

"Having a climbing buddy who was counting on me helped with the motivation to take my preparation very seriously," Tim said. "Without having that accountability, I would likely have delayed and delayed. Our Mt. Rainier story is a great example of how we accomplish bigger and better things together."

The cherry on top of the sundae was the special time Tim spent with Jon before he finished college. "I felt blessed to able to share that experience with my son," he said.

Gratitude

The final and most profound lesson of the Seven Fs can be summarized in one word: gratitude. Gratefulness wraps around each of the Seven Fs like a warm cotton robe. Gratefulness is the opposite of bitterness. Living gratefully every day creates an attractive mood that is contagious to others.

"We all get kicked in the teeth," explained a recently retired executive. "As I look back on my career, what I found to be irritating were the 'woe is me' people in my life who had a chip on their shoulders they couldn't shake off."

He talked of colleagues and team members who through the years had lost children in childbirth, endured cancer, or lost loved ones. He had friends go bankrupt and lose their businesses, and he's seen many families split up through divorce.

"What I cherish the most are the people who accept life's setback and have the ability to appreciate what they have—right here, right now—and to make the most of it," he said "Anyone can stay down when they get knocked over. The best people I know get back up and say 'I'm grateful to be standing today.'"

If you have $20 available to buy this book, you are wealthier than half of the world.

You probably know someone who suffered one of those hardships. It's possible you know someone who has been through them all. It might even be you!

Factually, anyone who is a college graduate and has a decent job, home, car, and a few prized possessions is more financially fortunate than about 98 percent of the people on this planet. And if you have $20 available to buy this book, you are wealthier than half of the world. If we can't find a way to feel grateful, then heaven help us!

Accepting the Challenge

If living gratefully is important, then why are some days so hard? Politicians, sociologists, and advertisers have driven the labels upper, middle, and lower class into our collective psyche, as if that's how we're predestined to live. More often than we care to admit, we pry open our wallets because someone has skillfully targeted our "class." Who isn't tempted by ads from Target, Nordstrom, Home Depot, or Royal Caribbean Cruises? If we aren't careful, our wish lists remind us of how much we don't have and that chip on our shoulder begins to grow.

The only real answer for how to fight back society's temptations is to know what you want. We hope you accept the challenge to dream without fear about the life you imagine. We hope you set clear, sharp, and compelling goals in each of the Seven Fs. Then with the help of friends and family, you can blend the Seven Fs together and live each day gratefully ever after.

Read on for how we believe the Seven Fs can work well in the workplace.

How Will the Seven Fs Play at Work?

If you've found the Seven Fs energizing and actionable in your personal life, we strongly suggest using the Seven Fs as a barometer of your business's vitality. As this Seven Fs project unfolded over the past twelve months, we found there are profound leadership benefits that accrue to those who lead based on a Seven Fs philosophy.

Following the Seven Fs creates a clearer path to a genuine leadership style which is perhaps the most in-demand attribute in leaders today. Whether we call it "humility," "sincerity," or "authenticity," followers today appreciate—and gravitate toward—leaders who are genuine and live a blended, holistic life. Leaders who match their words with their actions more easily earn genuine followers.

In this chapter, we make connections between each of the Seven Fs and how they might play out in your workplace. We also explore ideas that you may find specifically helpful at work.

Faith—Office Applications:
Mission | Values | Purpose | Social Good

You may not regularly think about it, but faith and spirituality are significant factors in the daily lives of many employees. Faith influences individual and corporate values, and these in turn shape the overarching culture of a workplace. If something is out of whack in a work culture, chances are good the disconnect is due to leadership expressing one set of values and acting out another. In the midst of our research, interviewees frequently noted "leadership hypocrisy" as a barrier to effective manager/employee communication and trust. Instead, employees noted their desire to see management's behavior move in lock-step with their employer's values.

> *Millennials—more than any other generation—would like their employers to act based on a clear sense of purpose.*

In particular, millennials—more than any other generation—like their employers to act based on a clear sense of purpose and a mission of social good. Millennials will often judge their engagement in organizations based on the three Is: their impact on the world, their level of independence and a distant third, income.

Core individual decisions about work, such as, "Can I really work here?" are fundamentally affected by faith. As we learned from Richard Davis in Chapter 1, faith profoundly influences our intuitive "gut feel" decision-making when the facts at hand don't provide a clear enough direction.

Chapter 1 references to faith as it applies to work:

- Chady AlAhmar story (page 22): Consider the importance of keeping work events in perspective to the difficulties of others.

- Dan Lieberman story (page 25): How might you involve your employees in expressing some of the most basic faith values with your customers and community?

- "The State of Faith" survey (page 27): Does it make sense to start or support a prayer group within your office or department?

Family—Office Applications:
Employee Loyalty | Corporate Culture

Among those who took the Seven Fs survey, family is consistently the highest priority and highest area of satisfaction. So it's safe to assume "family" is ever-present in the hearts and minds of our colleagues.

However, if we do things in the workplace like saying "family is important," but then frown on colleagues who volunteer their time at their kids' schools during work hours, we're eating away at our integrity. And leaders who refer to their corporate culture as a "family" are dangerously close to abusing an important metaphor. Families are based on unconditional love—employees don't really believe that applies to businesses.

Chapter 2 references to family as it applies to work:

- Vivek Agrawal story (page 36): How might you encourage colleagues to share stories about how they blend work and family to benefit others?

- Jill Schumann story (page 40): Have you collected success habits on how people can stay connected to family while on long trips?

- The *Wall Street Journal* story (page 46): How might you include employees' wedding anniversaries and other important family milestones in company news venues?

Finances—Office Applications:
Employee Well-being | Corporate Culture | Financial Stewardship

Finances is clearly the most common motivator of the Seven Fs, based on how we think about our work. That's consistent with the inherent expectations of managers and executives whose roles require them to be fiscally minded.

Most companies have a reasonable "do-not-discuss-compensation" code of conduct in the workplace. However, even though two out of three of our survey respondents say they are making as much or more money than they expected at this point in their lives, they also expressed significant dissatisfaction with their finances. Is it possible we aren't doing enough to promote financial prudence and literacy outside the workplace?

Programs to promote better financial literacy and planning help increase the probability our employees will feel grateful about their finances.

Chapter 3 references to finances as it relates to work:

- Professional woman who was laid off (page 50): How might employers help employees plan their monthly finances for maximum efficiency during good times, rather than waiting for a crisis to clean up their budgets at home?

- Jean Chatsky and Robert Emmons story (page 53): How can we think more gratefully when discussing finances at work?

- Fifty-something partner fixated on $3 million (page 54): How might we provide service to help senior professionals plan better to ensure they are not working out of fear or bitterness?

Fitness—Office Application:
Employee Health and Wellness | Corporate Culture

As our fitness improves, we feel better, sleep better, and bring more energy to work. Wellness programs are increasingly more popular as a piece of corporate culture, because they make good fiscal sense (lower health insurance costs, fewer sick days) and good creative sense (more innovation). There's a reason why General Mills has been promoting "Fitness Fridays" for more than twenty years: because it helps employees feel better about themselves and their work!

> There's a reason why General Mills has been promoting "Fitness Fridays" for more than twenty years.

Chapter 4 references to fitness as it applies to work:

- Dan Buettner story (page 67): How might you integrate exercise and nutritional fuel into the performance of your daily work? Does your work culture encourage employees to share lunch together, or are employees' schedules so jam-packed they're lucky to grab a quick bite at their desks?

- Meghan Huber story (page 71): What sort of exercise or sporting group could you start to engage other employees?

- Code RED explanation (page 74): How might you promote the concept of Code RED (reduction, education, and discipline) as cultural values within your workplace?

Friends—Office Application:
Employee Engagement | Culture and Building Alliances | Mentoring

Friends add significant value and satisfaction to our jobs and careers. Everyone knows college-educated and career-minded leaders spend more waking hours at work than at home. However, with our intense family commitments, we simply don't have much time outside of work for friends.

Does your culture encourage or discourage friendships at the office? Research confirmed friends at work help us be more productive and have better corporate attitudes. Friends help us endure the stress of our work lives in ways that keep us resilient, focused and sane. How do your leaders model the importance of friendships in the line of sight of your employees? How would a proactive mentoring program drive deep relationships and deeper accountability toward a common goal?

> *Research has confirmed friends at work help us be more productive.*

Chapter 5 references to friends as they apply to work:

- Gallup research mention (page 91): Do you have a best friend at work? If not, what's stopping you from finding one?

- Paul Koch story (page 93): Could you potentially do business with any of your friends? If so, what's stopping you?

- Facebook and social media tools mention (page 94): How might new social media tools help colleagues stay connected with one another?

Fun—Office Application:

Corporate Culture | Pride in the Organization Hiring, Recruiting and Retention

Fun in the workplace—or lack thereof—defines a significant part of an organization's soul. Leaders who encourage playfulness and joy at work have a contagious spirit that endures.

Recently, a group of 220 plus company leaders confirmed their organizations would be more satisfying places to work if "fun" was emphasized more in the workplace. Foosball and ping-pong tables are over-the-top clichés that might trigger the "snicker meter" in most office environments. However, there are other creative ways to have fun at work. If you seek to attract, retain and develop high-performing talent, doesn't it make sense to encourage a little more fun at the office?

Chapter 6 references to fun as it applies to work:

- Mocha Monkey coffee shop story (page 102): Is there a fun hangout at work or off site employees can share?

- Bowling with the sales team story (page 110): Is there a fun activity with which you can engage multiple employees?

- Noel Raymond engaging Pillsbury Neighborhood Services employees in ways to make the workplace fun (page 111): Are there intentional things you could do in the workplace to have more fun?

Future—Office Application:

Mission | Vision | Recruiting and Hiring | Corporate Giving | Big Hairy Audacious Goals

Future is about the mission and vision of your enterprise. Employees, investors, and business partners want to know the answers to these simple questions: "Where are we going?" and "How will we recognize if we are making progress?" Future is about the hope we have for ourselves and others.

> *Leaders believe more emphasis on the future would make their workplace more satisfying.*

Among survey respondents, future finished second only to fun for current satisfaction. Our own research confirmed leaders believe more emphasis on the future would make their workplace more satisfying. However, most companies contribute generously to charities and causes—i.e., investing in the future of others—without telling their employees about it. At the very least, doesn't it make sense to publish an annual giving report to build company pride by articulating the time, energy, and money your organization has collectively given to future-oriented causes?

Chapter 7 references to future as it applies to work:

- TOMS Shoes story (page 125): Could your company do more to encourage the future good of others?

- Oak Grove Middle School story (page 119): How can we encourage employees to volunteer in schools and/or organizations educating and training our leaders of the future?

- Rotary story (page 125): How can you encourage employees to participate in service clubs such as Rotary and others?

Each of the Seven Fs contributes to what the highest-performing organizations strive to achieve. Specifically, they work to increase trust in leadership and create a happier and healthier employee base, which establishes deeper relationships with customers and results in achieving the business satisfaction and profitability you imagine.

It's relatively simple to see how happier and healthier employees increase our probability of success and deliver a more positive impact on our communities. But why should customers care about the Seven Fs?

The answer resides in the fact that price and technology advantages (features and benefits) are becoming less and less effective in sustaining good customer relationships. Buyers expect high quality and our best price as ante to the business poker game. And we are seeing an increase in how corporate profits are invested back in the community for social good.

What most customers really want today is excellent service delivered by organizations that genuinely care about the success of their customers, and have a positive impact on their communities. Building relationships around the Seven Fs will help your organization build goodwill with customers to help withstand the inevitable ups and downs of economic and innovation cycles.

Finally, leaders themselves benefit the most from adopting a Seven Fs perspective. For better or worse, we are living in an increasingly open society, in which information technology is leveling traditional top-down, "because-I-said-so" workplace cultures. Leaders who openly share what's on their minds with humility and openness will endear themselves to their employees, customers, and shareholders. Those who lead their work and home lives with consistently visible Seven Fs values will undoubtedly receive the benefit of the doubt in both their hiring and retention decisions.

Connect with the authors:

Paul Batz: paul@goodleadership.com
Tim Schmidt: timschmidt.sevenfs@gmail.com

Seven Fs
Inspiration
in your
Inbox
once a week!

Get the Good Leadership Blog, by Paul Batz

Paul Batz is founder and president of Good Leadership Enterprises. He is an inspirational leadership coach, best selling author and professional speaker. His Good Leadership blog is recognized as one of the top leadership posts in America. Enjoy his first e-book: *Good Leadership Today*.

Chapter 2

Who needs your help today?

Good leaders make a habit of letting instincts take over, even when self-responsibility is front-of-mind. And we are willing to take the risk of helping others, even when it multiplies the pressure of our day.

"I'm terribly lost," she said frantically with cloudy, 84 year-old eyes. *"Can you help me?"*

Nancy and I met last week at the Minneapolis/St. Paul airport, at the south terminal gate security. I was focused and selfishly absorbed in my workday, preparing to race through TSA Pre-Check on my way to Los Angeles for business. Nancy, whom I had never met before, was dazed and confused—walking in circles, trying to find the plane to Denver that would take her to celebrate Thanksgiving with her grandchildren.

When our eyes met, we shared a compelling mission.

Our flights were scheduled to leave at the same time—just 32 minutes from then, on opposite ends of the airport. As an experienced traveler, I knew passengers were already pre-boarding both planes. By helping Nancy, I added significant risk to catching my L.A. plane on time.

"I don't know where I need to be," she pleaded. *"I have my boarding pass, but I need to check this luggage,"* she explained. Even though we were less than 20 yards from the South security station, bags like hers can only be checked at the North security station. Without thinking, "Come with me, I'll help you!" came out of my mouth.

Visions of the 1980s O.J. Simpson Hertz commercials flashed through my head: *we need to run,* I thought. Oh yeah: *she can't run.* I smiled to myself at the challenge: *What have I gotten myself into?*

Escalators can seem gruelingly slow when you are in a hurry to get through airport security.

Our 84-year-old sprint/walk was rewarded when the elevator opened before I even pressed the button. On the Tram Level, we boarded the train without a wait (that never happens). Eventually, we were inserting her passport into the luggage tag scanner. A Delta attendant noticed our frenzy and bypassed the other travelers to help us (that seldom happens). As Nancy's bag was successfully tagged, the nice Delta lady said: *"Nancy, your plane leaves in less than 15 minutes from Terminal F. I believe you can make it if you hurry."*

That's good news, except neither of us had been through security yet.

"At least at my age, I get to go through the fast lane *in security,"* Nancy attempted to soften the tension. "Me too," I smiled. We trotted into our brisk 84-year-old-lady pace and stepped onto the escalator to the Ticketing Level. On the way up, she sighed, look straight into my eyes and said: *"I'm going to call my daughter when I get on the plane and tell her I met an angel today."*

"Thank you, and Happy Thanksgiving!" Nancy said as we parted after security.

As I write this Thanksgiving story, I have no proof Nancy got onto her plane in time: I ran to my gate—feeling young, strong and calm. All I know is, my butt hit the seat just three minutes before they shut the passenger door. I stared out the oval window into the grey November sky and thought: *"She's going to call her daughter when she gets on the plane and tell her she met an angel today. . . . "*

This morning, I'm grateful because *I just met another person I want to be when I grow up.* What a gift! Will I have the wealth, courage and adventurous spirit to travel by myself when I'm 84 years old? Will I be humble and candid enough to ask for help, when I need it? I hope so.

Good leaders make a habit of letting instincts take over even when self-responsibility is in the front of minds. And we are willing to take the risk of helping others, even when it multiplies the pressure of our day.

Will you have the wealth, courage and adventurous spirit to travel when you are 84 years old?]

 Reflection:

How will I recognize when someone really needs my help today?

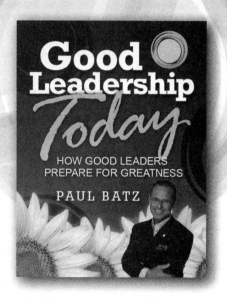

About the Authors

© 2011 Clare Pix Photography

Tim Schmidt and **Paul Batz** are devoted family men, entrepreneurs and executives who share their insights about how successful people live with less stress and lead with less fear. What they've learned is both simple and profound...and it can really work for you.

"Paul and Tim have written a wonderful, thought-provoking book on blending what's most important in our lives. A more balanced life is exactly what most of us need and want."
Paul Harmel, chairman and CEO of Lifetouch